HORS D'OEUVRES

HORS D'OEUVRES

Eric Treuille and Victoria Blashford-Snell

PHOTOGRAPHY BY IAN O'LEARY

LONDON, NEW YORK, MELBOURNE,
MUNICH, and DELHI

US Team
SENIOR EDITOR
Barbara Berger
EDITORIAL ASSISTANT
Phil Poyer
RECIPE CONSULTANTS
Wesley Martin
Barbara Bowman, Gourmetsleuth
EDITORIAL CONSULTANT
Jane Perlmutter
DTP DESIGNER
Milos Orlovic

UK Team
MANAGING EDITOR
Stephanie Farrow
DTP DESIGNER
Sonia Charbonnier
EDITORIAL CONSULTANT
Rosie Kindersley
DESIGN AND ART DIRECTION
Stuart Jackman
PROJECT EDITOR
Julia Pemberton Hellums
ASSISTANT EDITOR
Sally Somers
PRODUCTION CONTROLLER
Elizabeth Cherry
INDEXER
Valerie Lewis Chandler
FOOD STYLING
Eric Treuillé

DEDICATION
To my wife.
To my husband.

Second American Edition 2004
2 4 6 8 10 9 7 5 3 1

Published in the United States by
DK Publishing Inc.,
375 Hudson Street, New York, New York 10014

DK Publishing, Inc. offers special discounts for bulk
purchases for sales promotions or premiums. Specific, large-quantity needs can be met
with special editions, including personalized covers, excerpts of existing guides, and
corporate imprints. For more information, contact: Special Markets Department,
DK Publishing, Inc.,
375 Hudson Street, New York, NY 10014
Fax: 212-689-5254

Cataloging-in-Publication Data
is available from the Library of Congress

ISBN 0-7566-0371-4

Color reproduction in Italy by GRB
Printed and bound by L. Rex Printing Company Ltd, China.

Discover more at
www.dk.com

CONTENTS

INTRODUCTION

From the simplest to the grandest party, entertaining means sharing. Since time immemorial, the traditional way to express friendship has been with an open house, a warm welcome, and good food lovingly prepared. We were fortunate enough to grow up in households where home cooked meals were a pleasurable ritual that punctuated our lives. Then, we learned the joy of connecting with family and friends over food. Now, many people don't seem to have the time or the energy to cook, let alone entertain, at home. The constraints of modern life call for a new approach to entertaining. "Can I make that ahead?" is the question we are most often asked at the cooking classes we teach.

An hors d'oeuvres party is a practical way for both experienced and beginner cooks to entertain at home. A large number of guests can be accommodated without matching dinner service, tables, or even chairs. Piles of dirty pans, plates, and cutlery cluttering up the sink are not a burden, because hors d'oeuvres are easily handheld and simply eaten with only a small paper napkin. There's no need to worry about spending all day or all night in the kitchen. Hors d'oeuvres are flexible foods that can be prepared well ahead of time.

We set out to create a cookbook that puts the pleasure back into entertaining. We have included practical tips, techniques, and timing that we hope will inspire you to invite your friends and family to celebrate.

We don't want to turn home cooks into professional caterers. We want to help home cooks be confident cooks, because confident cooks make happy hosts, and happy hosts give great parties.

So, relax. Because everybody loves a party, and home-cooked food always makes an occasion special.

Eric   Aurora

NOTES FROM THE COOKS

BEFORE YOU COOK read through the recipe carefully. Make sure you have all the equipment and ingredients required.

ON MEASURING

Accurate measurements are essential if you want the same good results each time you make a recipe.

We recommend using cook's measuring spoons when following a recipe. All spoon measurements in the book are level unless otherwise stated. To measure dry ingredients with a spoon, scoop the ingredient lightly from the storage container, then level the surface with the edge of a straight-bladed knife.

We use standard level spoon measurements
1 tbsp = ½ floz
1 tsp = ⅙ floz

For maximum accuracy when using graduated measuring cups for dry ingredients, spoon the ingredient loosely into the required cup, mounding it up slightly, then level the surface with the edge of a straight-bladed knife. Do not use the cup as a scoop, pack the ingredient into the cup or tap the cup on the work surface. This will give you an inaccurate result.

To measure liquids, choose a transparent glass or plastic measuring jug. Always place the jug on a flat surface and check for accuracy at eye level when pouring in a liquid to measure.

A final and important rule of measuring—never measure ingredients over the mixing bowl!

ON OVEN TEMPERATURES

Always preheat your oven for 10–20 minutes before you need to use it. This allows it to reach the required temperature. Keep in mind that the higher the temperature required, the longer it will take to preheat the oven.

Ovens vary from kitchen to kitchen. Most have hot spots, so be prepared to rotate dishes from top to bottom or from front to back during the cooking time. A good oven thermometer is an important piece of kitchen equipment.

If using a convection oven, follow the manufacturer's instructions for adjusting cooking timings and oven temperatures.

ON QUANTITIES

However accurate we measure, cooking remains to some extent an unpredictable science. Ingredients vary, so use the yields we give for each recipe as general guidelines. Hors D'oeuvres are bite-size morsels that should be eaten in one mouthful, so be prepared to modify the number of items the recipe yields to fit this criteria. We have done our best to ensure that none of the recipes yield less than the quantity stated, but in some cases a recipe might make a few extra, which will of course allow for both breakage—and tasting!

ON TASTING

Always taste food as you cook and before you serve. Don't be afraid to add or change flavors to suit your palate—what's fun about cooking is experimenting, improvising, creating. Ingredients differ from day to day, season to season, kitchen to kitchen; our tomato may be a little riper than your tomato, and so on. Be prepared to the adjust sweetness, sharpness, spiciness, and, most important of all, salt to your own taste.

STORE-BOUGHT FOR GETTING AHEAD

Make use of store-bought bases, cases, and sauces to save time and relieve preparty pressure.
Look for these at gourmet stores and in larger supermarkets.

1. Mayonnaise
2. Bouchée cases
3. Chocolate cups
4. Croustades
5. Filo pastry
6. Horseradish sauce
7. Puff pastry
8. Pesto
9. Pastry cases
10. Flour tortillas

FINE FOODS FOR SPECIAL OCCASIONS

Celebrations call for a little luxury. Indulge family and friends with ingredients of the highest quality and throw in some of these gourmet treats.

1. Parmesan cheese
2. Stilton cheese
3. Roquefort cheese
4. Quail eggs
5. Lobster
6. Black lumpfish roe
7. Red lumpfish roe
8. Salmon roe
9. Caviar
10. Medium shrimp
11. Tiger shrimp
12. Bay scallops
13. Sea scallops
14. Crab claw
15. Smoked salmon
16. Proscuitto
17. Oyster

BOLD FLAVORS FOR BITE-SIZED MORSELS

Hors d'oeuvres are tiny mouthfuls of food designed to stimulate the appetite and whet the thirst. Raid the global pantry for sweet, sharp, spicy, salty, and sour flavors and remember to season with a generous hand.

1 Lemon, lime, and orange zest
2 Thai sweet chili sauce
3 Chinese hot chili sauce
4 Tabasco
5 Balsamic vinegar
6 Worcestershire sauce
7 Curry powder
8 Paprika

9 Crushed red pepper flakes
10 Cayenne
11 Sesame seeds
12 Pickled ginger
13 Horseradish sauce
14 Olives
15 Anchovy fillets
16 Chipotes in adobo

17 Grainy mustard
18 Mustard powder
19 Dijon mustard
20 Chili peppers
21 Fresh herbs
22 Baby capers
23 Capers

KITCHEN TOOLS

A good, sharp knife, a selection of pastry cutters, a melon baller, and a piping bag with tubes will create myriad professional-looking hors d'oeuvres.

1. 1-inch fluted pastry cutter
2. 2-inch fluted pastry cutter
3. 1¾-inch fluted pastry cutter
4. 2¾-inch plain pastry cutter
5. 2-inch plain pastry cutter
6. 1½-inch plain pastry cutter
7. 2½-inch star-shaped pastry cutter
8. 2½-inch heart-shaped cutter

9. 1½-inch heart-shaped pastry cutter
10. Vegetable peeler
11. Oyster knife
12. Melon baller
13. Zester
14. Olive pitter
15. Serrated knife
16. Chef's knife
17. Kitchen scissors
18. Large star piping tip
19. Large plain piping tip

1 Plain tartlet tin
2 Baking sheet
3 Mini muffin tins
4 Fluted tartlet tins
5 Sheet pan

BAKEWARE

Flat baking sheets, rimmed sheet pans, and mini muffin tins are the most essential bakeware in the hors d'oeuvre kitchen. Continental tartlet tins are a bonus, since they make the daintiest pastry cases, but mini muffin tins work well too.

THE RECIPES

READ THROUGH THE RECIPE FIRST.

USE FRESH SEASONAL INGREDIENTS.

HAVE FUN—YOU'RE COOKING FOR A PARTY.

Nibbles, Dips, and Dippers

SPICED PARTY NUTS

MAKES 2 CUPS

2 cups blanched almonds
1 tbsp egg white, about ½ an egg white
2 tsp dark brown sugar
2 tsp salt
½ tsp cayenne pepper
1 tbsp finely chopped rosemary leaves

Preheat oven to 300°F.
Spread nuts in a single layer on a sheet pan. Roast, shaking the tray occasionally, until lightly golden, 15 minutes. Remove from oven and cool slightly. Beat egg white until frothy and add nuts, sugar, salt, cayenne, and rosemary. Toss ingredients together to coat each nut well. Return nuts to the oven. Roast until fragrant and golden, 20 minutes. Cool. Serve at room temperature.

THINK AHEAD
Make up to 3 days in advance. Cool and store in an airtight container at room temperature. Alternatively, freeze up to 1 month in advance (see page 149). Defrost overnight in refrigerator. Crisp in a preheated 350°F oven, 3 minutes.

COOKS' NOTE
To make curried almonds omit sugar, cayenne, and rosemary and replace with 1 tbsp curry powder.

CRUNCHY SWEET AND SPICY PECANS

MAKES 2 CUPS

2 cups pecans
1 tbsp sunflower oil
4 tbsp sugar
1 tsp salt
1½ tsp chili powder

Preheat oven to 300°F.
Spread pecans on a sheet pan. Roast, shaking the tray occasionally, until toasted, 30 minutes. Heat the oil in a frying pan over medium heat. Add nuts and stir to coat. Sprinkle with sugar and salt. Cook, stirring constantly, until the sugar melts and starts to brown slightly, 5 minutes. Remove from heat but continue stirring until nuts have cooled slightly. Sprinkle with chili powder and toss to coat each nut well. Serve at room temperature.

THINK AHEAD
Make up to 3 days in advance. Cool and store in an airtight container at room temperature. Alternatively, freeze up to 1 month in advance (see page 149). Defrost overnight in refrigerator. Crisp in a preheated 350°F oven, 3 minutes.

COOKS' NOTE
Use the variety of chili powders now available at gourmet food shops to achieve slightly different flavors. Ancho chilli powder will add a hint of smoky flavor to this piquant mixture.

MEDITERRANEAN MARINATED OLIVES

MAKES 2 CUPS

2 cups black or green olives
** or a mixture**
1 tsp fennel seeds
½ tsp cumin seeds
grated zest of ½ orange
grated zest of ½ lemon
2 garlic cloves, finely chopped
2 tsp crushed red pepper flakes
1 tsp dried oregano
1 tbsp lemon juice
1 tbsp red wine vinegar
2 tbsp olive oil
1 tbsp finely chopped parsley leaves

If desired, pit olives. Toast fennel and cumin seeds in an ungreased pan over low heat until aromatic, 2 minutes. Combine seeds, olives, zest, garlic, red pepper, oregano, lemon, vinegar, and oil and toss to coat each olive well. Place in an airtight container. Let marinate at room temperature for 8 hours. Shake the container occasionally to remix the ingredients while marinating. Stir in the parsley. Serve at room temperature.

THINK AHEAD
Make up to 1 week in advance, omitting the parsley. Store in an airtight container and refrigerate. Add parsley up to 3 hours before serving.

COOKS' NOTE
Warming the olives will intensify the flavors. Gently heat the marinated olives over a low heat until warmed through, 5 minutes. Serve warm.

SAVORY SABLES

MAKES 40

2 cups all-purpose flour	**¼ tsp mustard powder**
12 tbsp cold butter, diced	**1 egg yolk beaten with**
½ lb Gruyère cheese, grated	**1 tbsp water**
¼ tsp cayenne pepper	

ESSENTIAL EQUIPMENT
2½-inch star-shaped pastry cutter, 2½-inch heart-shaped pastry cutter, baking parchment

Place flour, butter, cheese, cayenne, and mustard powder in a food processor; pulse until the mixture forms a pastry. Add a little cold water (1 tsp at a time) as necessary to bring the pastry together.

Roll out pastry on a floured surface to a ¼-inch thickness. Stamp out into decorative shapes with pastry cutters. Place ¾ inch apart on 2 baking parchment-lined baking sheets. Refrigerate cut pastry shapes until firm, 30 minutes.

Preheat oven to 350°F.

Bake until golden brown, 10 minutes. Cool on a wire rack.

Serve warm or at room temperature, with or without dips.

THINK AHEAD
Make sablés up to 2 weeks in advance. Store in an airtight container at room temperature. Alternatively, make and freeze up to 1 month in advance (see page 149). Defrost and crisp for 3 minutes in preheated 400°F oven.

FLAVORED SABLE VARIATIONS

SPICY SABLES
Place 2 tsp paprika with the other ingredients in the food processor.

SEEDED SABLES
Omit mustard powder. Place 2 tsp caraway seeds with the other ingredients in the food processor.

HERBED SABLES
Omit mustard powder. Place 2 tsp finely chopped rosemary leaves with the other ingredients in the food processor.

ROQUEFORT SABLES
Omit mustard powder and cayenne. Use a combination of 4oz crumbled Roquefort cheese and 4oz grated Gruyère instead of 8oz grated Gruyère.

SWISS CHEESE ALLUMETTES

MAKES 30
1 cup all-purpose flour
6 tbsp cold butter, diced
1 egg yolk
¼ cup grated Gruyère cheese
salt, black pepper, cayenne pepper
1 egg beaten with 1 tbsp water
1 tbsp grated Parmesan cheese

ESSENTIAL EQUIPMENT
baking parchment

Place flour, butter, egg yolk, and cheese with a pinch each of salt, pepper, and cayenne in a food processor; pulse until the mixture forms a firm pastry. Turn out and knead lightly by hand until smooth.

Roll out pastry on a floured surface to a ¼ inch thickness. Cut into strips about ½-inch wide and 3 inches long. Place ¾ inch apart on baking parchment-lined baking sheets. Refrigerate until firm, 30 minutes.

Preheat oven to 350°F.

Brush with beaten egg. Sprinkle with Parmesan. Bake until golden brown, 15 minutes. Cool on a wire rack.

Serve warm or at room temperature, with or without dips.

THINK AHEAD
Make allumettes up to 2 weeks in advance. Store in an airtight container at room temperature. Alternatively, make and freeze up to 1 month in advance (see page 149). Defrost and crisp for 3 minutes in preheated 400°F oven.

PARMESAN AND PINE NUT BISCOTTINI WITH GREEN OLIVES

MAKES 50

¾ **cup pine nuts**
2 **cups all-pupose flour**
1 **tsp baking powder**
1 **tsp salt**
¼ **tsp black pepper**
1 **tbsp fennel seeds**
2 **tbsp grated Parmesan cheese**
1 **cup medium pitted green olives,**
  finely chopped
3 **eggs, beaten**

Preheat oven to 350°F. Spread pine nuts in a single layer on an oven tray. Toast in oven until golden, 7 minutes. Cool. Sift flour, baking powder, and salt into a bowl. Add pepper, fennel seeds, Parmesan, olives, and eggs and mix with a fork to form a rough dough. Alternatively, place flour, baking powder, salt, pepper, fennel seeds, Parmesan, olives, and eggs in a food processor; pulse to a rough dough. Knead the pine nuts into the dough with hands. Divide dough into 4 equal-sized pieces. Shape each piece into a log, 1 inch thick and 12 inches long. Place each log on a floured baking sheet. Bake until firm to the touch, 25 minutes. Remove and leave until cool enough to handle. With a serrated knife, cut each biscotti log on the diagonal into ½-inch-thick slices. Place the slices in a single layer on the baking sheets. Bake until crisp and dry, 15 minutes. Cool completely on a wire rack.

THINK AHEAD
Make up to 2 weeks in advance. Store in an airtight container at room temperature. Alternatively, freeze the unbaked biscotti logs up to 1 month in advance (see page 149). Defrost overnight in the refrigerator before baking.

TRIPLE CHOCOLATE BISCOTTINI WITH HAZELNUTS

MAKES 50

1⅔ **cups all-purpose flour**
⅔ **cup cocoa powder**
¾ **tsp baking powder**
¼ **tsp salt**
¾ **cup superfine sugar**

2oz **dark chocolate, chopped**
3 **eggs, beaten**
1 **tsp vanilla extract**
1 **cup hazelnuts, skinned**
  (see page 163)
3½oz **white chocolate to garnish**

ESSENTIAL EQUIPMENT
paper piping bag (see page 146)

Preheat oven 350°F.
Sift flour, cocoa, baking powder, and salt into a bowl. Add sugar, chocolate, eggs, and vanilla and mix with a fork to form a rough dough. Alternatively, place flour, cocoa, baking powder, salt, sugar, chocolate, eggs, and vanilla in a food processor; pulse to form a rough dough.
By hand, knead the hazelnuts into the dough. Divide the dough into 4 equal-sized pieces. Shape each piece into logs, 1 inch thick and 12 inches long. Place logs on floured baking sheets. Bake until firm to the touch, 25 minutes. Remove and leave until cool enough to handle. With a serrated knife, cut each biscotti log on the diagonal into ½-inch-thick slices. Place the slices in a single layer on baking sheets. Bake until crisp and dry, 15 minutes. Cool on a wire rack. Melt the white chocolate (see page 145) and drizzle, with a spoon, over the biscottini.

THINK AHEAD
Make up to 2 weeks in advance. Store in an airtight container at room temperature. Alternatively, freeze the unbaked biscotti logs up to 1 month in advance (see page 149). Defrost overnight in the refrigerator before baking.

COOKS' NOTE
For an alternative finish, try dipping one end of each biscottini into the melted white chocolate.

CURRY PUFFS

MAKES 35

1 recipe unbaked choux pastry
  (see page 138)
1 tsp cumin seeds
2 tsp curry powder
1 tsp turmeric
¼ tsp cayenne pepper
½ onion, grated

Preheat oven to 350°F.
Toast cumin seeds in an ungreased pan over low heat until fragrant, 3 minutes. Stir toasted spices and onion into pastry. Drop teaspoonfuls onto a greased baking sheet. Bake until golden, 30 minutes. Serve warm.

THINK AHEAD
Bake up to 3 days in advance. Store in an airtight container at room temperature. Crisp in preheated 400°F oven, 3 minutes.
Alternatively, bake and freeze up to 1 month in advance (see page 149). Defrost. Crisp as directed.

CHORIZO PUFFS

MAKES 35

¼ lb chorizo sausage, casing removed and finely chopped
1 recipe unbaked choux pastry
(see page 138)

Preheat oven to 350°F.
Stir chorizo into pastry. Drop teaspoonfuls onto a greased baking sheet. Bake until golden, 30 minutes. Serve warm.

THINK AHEAD
Bake up to 3 days in advance. Store in an airtight container at room temperature. Crisp in preheated 400°F oven, 3 minutes.
Alternatively, bake and freeze up to 1 month in advance (see page 149). Defrost. Crisp as directed.

MINI GOUGERES

MAKES 30

1 cup grated Gruyère cheese
1 recipe unbaked choux pastry
(see page 138)

ESSENTIAL EQUIPMENT
piping bag with large, plain tube

Preheat oven to 350°F.
Stir half of the cheese into the pastry. Fill piping bag with pastry (see page 146) and pipe out rings, each one about 2 inches in diameter, onto an oiled baking sheet. Sprinkle with remaining cheese. Bake until golden, 30 minutes. Serve warm.

THINK AHEAD
Bake up to 3 days in advance. Store in an airtight container at room temperature. Crisp in preheated 400°F oven, 3 minutes.
Alternatively, bake and freeze up to 1 month in advance (see page 149). Defrost. Crisp as directed.

PARMESAN AND ANCHOVY PALMIERS

MAKES 20

1 sheet puff pastry
1¾ oz drained anchovy fillets, finely chopped
¼ tsp black pepper
2 tbsp grated Parmesan cheese
1 egg yolk beaten with 1 tbsp water

Preheat oven to 400°F.
Roll pastry to a 6 x 14-inch rectangle. Trim uneven edges with a sharp knife. Spread anchovies evenly over pastry. Sprinkle with pepper and Parmesan. Roll up ends tightly to meet in the middle of pastry (see below). Refrigerate until firm, 20 minutes. Brush with beaten egg on all sides. Cut across into ½-inch-thick slices. Place slices on a greased baking sheet. Bake until crisp and golden, 10 minutes. Cool on wire rack. Serve warm or at room temperature.

THINK AHEAD
Same as recipes opposite.

Rolling up pastry for palmiers.

SUN-DRIED TOMATO PESTO PALMIERS

MAKES 20

6 sun-dried tomatoes in oil, drained (reserve oil), and finely chopped
1 garlic clove, crushed
1 tbsp reserved oil from sun-dried tomatoes
3 tbsp grated Parmesan cheese
1 sheet puff pastry
1 egg yolk beaten with 1 tbsp water

Preheat oven to 400°F.
For pesto, mix tomatoes, garlic, reserved oil, and 2 tbsp Parmesan until well combined. Roll pastry to 6 x 14-inch rectangle. Trim uneven edges with sharp knife. Spread pesto evenly over pastry. Roll up ends tightly to meet in the middle of pastry (see below, left). Refrigerate until firm, 20 minutes. Brush with beaten egg on all sides. Cut crosswise into ½-inch-thick slices. Place slices on a greased baking sheet. Bake until crisp and golden, 10 minutes. Sprinkle with remaining Parmesan when hot from oven. Cool on wire rack. Serve warm or at room temperature.

THINK AHEAD
Bake up to 3 days in advance. Crisp in preheated 400°F, 3 minutes. Store in an airtight container at room temperature. Alternatively, freeze unbaked (see page 149). Bake frozen in preheated 200°F for 15 minutes.

HONEY MUSTARD AND PROSCIUTTO PALMIERS

MAKES 20

1 sheet puff pastry
2 tsp Dijon mustard
4 tsp honey
2½ oz sliced prosciutto
3 tbsp grated Parmesan cheese
1 egg yolk beaten with 1 tbsp water

Preheat oven to 400°F.
Roll pastry to a 6 x 14-inch rectangle. Trim uneven edges with sharp knife. Combine mustard and honey. Spread evenly over pastry. Cover with sliced prosciutto. Sprinkle with 2 tbsp Parmesan. Roll up ends tightly to meet in the middle of pastry (see below, far left). Refrigerate until firm, 20 minutes. Brush with beaten egg on all sides. Cut across into ½-inch slices. Place slices on a greased baking sheet. Bake until crisp and golden, 10 minutes. Sprinkle over remaining Parmesan when hot from oven. Cool on wire rack. Serve warm or at room temperature.

THINK AHEAD
Bake up to 3 days in advance. Crisp in preheated 400°F, 3 minutes. Store in an airtight container at room temperature. Alternatively, freeze unbaked (see page 149). Bake from frozen in preheated 400°F for 15 minutes.

TWISTED PARSLEY BREADSTICKS

MAKES 35

1 recipe unbaked bread dough
  (see page 140)
1 cup shredded sharp cheddar cheese
1 cup flat-leaf parsley leaves, roughly
  chopped
¼ tsp cayenne pepper

Preheat oven to 400°F.
Roll out dough to a 6 x 20-inch rectangle.
Sprinkle with cheese, parsley, and
cayenne. Fold dough in half crosswise.
Roll dough lightly to press in the filling
and compress the two layers together.
With a sharp knife, cut dough crosswise
into ¼-inch-wide strips. Hold ends of
each strip between your fingers and
twist ends in opposite directions. Lay
twisted strips onto greased baking
sheets (see below). Bake until crisp and
golden, 15 minutes. Cool on wire rack.
Serve warm or at room temperature.

THINK AHEAD
Bake up to 3 days in advance. Store in an airtight
container at room temperature. Crisp in preheated
400°F oven, 3 minutes.

PARMESAN CHEESE STRAWS

MAKES 40

1 sheet puff pastry
2 tsp paprika
3 tbsp grated Parmesan cheese
1 egg yolk beaten with 1 tbsp water

Preheat oven to 400°F.
Roll out pastry to a 6 x 20-inch rectangle.
Sprinkle over paprika and 2 tbsp of the
Parmesan. Spread cheese with your
hands to evenly cover pastry. Fold
pastry in half widthways. Brush folded
pastry with beaten egg. Sprinkle with
remaining Parmesan. Press lightly
into the pastry with hands to secure
the cheese.
With a sharp knife, cut pastry crosswise
into ¼-inch-wide strips. Hold ends of
each strip between your fingers and
twist ends in opposite directions (see
below, left). Lay twisted strips onto
greased baking sheets. Bake until
crisp and golden, 7 minutes. Cool
on wire racks. Serve warm or at
room temperature.

THINK AHEAD
Bake up to 3 days in advance. Store in airtight
container at room temperature. Crisp in preheated
400°F oven, 3 minutes.

VEGETABLE DIPPERS

Prepare your chosen vegetables as
directed. Arrange vegetables in an
airtight container covered with damp
paper towels. Cover with the lid and
refrigerate. Serve chilled, with dips.

BABY CARROTS Choose firm, crisp
baby carrots and use as quickly as
possible since they spoil more quickly
than regular carrots. Do not peel. Trim
root end but leave a short green stem
to act as a handle for dipping.

BABY POTATOES Choose even-sized,
small new potatoes with a crisp, waxy
texture and papery, thin skins.
Simmer, unpeeled, in salted water
until tender when pierced with the tip
of a small sharp knife. Use both gold-
and red-skinned potatoes for added
color contrast.

CARROTS Avoid large carrots sicne
they may have a tough, woody core.
Organically grown carrots have the
sweetest flavor. Cut into sticks about
3 inches long and ¼ inch thick.

CELERY Use only the pale, tender
inner stalks. The outer stalks tend to
be stringy and should be peeled. Cut
into sticks about 3-inches long and
¼ inch thick.

CHICORY Trim the bitter stem end
and use only the crisp, smaller inner
leaves. Chicory is grown in red as well
as white varieties.

CHERRY TOMATOES Try to find yellow
as well as red for color contrast. The
plum- and pear-shaped cherry tomato
varieties are now widely available.
Their elongated shape makes them
easier to use for dipping.

CUCUMBERS Scrape out the seeds
and discard. Cut into sticks about
3 inches long and ¼ inch thick. Leave
unpeeled for added color contrast
between the dark green peel and
pearly pale green interior.

RADISHES Trim the root end but
leave a little green stem on to act as a
handle for dipping. Elongated
French-style varieties with red tops
and white tips are best for dipping.

THINK AHEAD
Prepare vegetables up to 1 day in advance.

COOKS' NOTE
A generous quantity of just one or two vegetables
makes an impressive display. Choose vegetables
that are at their freshest, seasonal best, rather
than aiming for a lavish selection.

FORMING TWISTED STRIPS
Twist ends in opposite directions

OVEN-DRIED ROOT AND FRUIT CHIPS

MAKES ABOUT 3 CUPS
1 small sweet potato, unpeeled
1 small beet, unpeeled
1 small parsnip, unpeeled
1 apple, unpeeled
1 pear, unpeeled
2 tsp salt

ESSENTIAL EQUIPMENT
either a food processor with a slicing attachment, a mandoline or a Japanese vegetable slicer

Preheat oven to 350°F.
Use either the slicing attachment on a food processor, mandoline, or Japanese vegetable slicer to slice the unpeeled sweet potato, beet, parsnip, apple, and pear ⅛ inch thick. Place slices in a single layer on oiled baking sheets. Put into the oven. Reduce oven temperature to 250°F. Bake for 1½ hours, turning the slices over every 20 minutes, until dried. Cool in single layers on wire racks. Sprinkle with salt. Serve at room temperature, with or without dips.

THINK AHEAD
Make up to 1 day in advance. Store in an airtight container at room temperature.

CRISPY POTATO SKINS

MAKES 40
5 medium potatoes, pricked
2 tbsp olive oil
1 tbsp finely chopped fresh rosemary leaves
  or 2 tsp crumbled dried rosemary
1½ tsp salt
1 tsp black pepper

Preheat oven to 350°F.
Bake potatoes until tender, 1 hour. Cool. Cut each potato into 6 wedges. Scoop out the cooked potato, leaving the skins intact and a shell of potato and skin, about ¼ inch thick. If desired, reserve cooked potato for another use.
Brush potato skins with oil on both sides. Place in a single layer scooped side up onto a wire rack set on top of an oven tray. Sprinkle evenly with rosemary, salt, and pepper. Bake for 15 minutes, then remove from oven and turn skins over. Return skins to the oven and continue baking until crisp and golden brown, 15 minutes. Serve at room temperature, with or without dips.

THINK AHEAD
Make up to 1 day in advance. Store in an airtight container at room temperature.

COOKS' NOTE
Make this recipe the day before your party and use the reserved cooked potato to make delicious mashed potatoes for dinner the night before.

HERBED PITA CRISPS

MAKES 40
2 garlic cloves, crushed
6 tbsp olive oil
4 pita breads, white or whole wheat
2 tbsp fresh thyme leaves
  or 2 tsp dried thyme
1½ tsp salt
1 tsp black pepper

ESSENTIAL EQUIPMENT
kitchen scissors or a serrated knife

Preheat oven to 350°F.
Stir garlic into oil. Cut each pita into 5 strips with scissors or a serrated knife. Snip end of each strip and separate to make 2 single-layer strips. Place pita strips split side up in a single layer on baking sheets. Brush with garlic olive oil. Sprinkle evenly with thyme, salt, and pepper. Bake until crisp and golden brown, 15 minutes. Cool. Serve at room temperature with or without dips.

THINK AHEAD
Make up to 2 days in advance. Store in an airtight container at room temperature.

COOKS' NOTE
To make spiced pita crisps, sprinkle pita with 2 tsp each cumin and sesame seeds instead of thyme leaves.

CHICKEN DRUMMETTES

20 chicken wings

ESSENTIAL EQUIPMENT
kitchen scissors or sharp boning knife

Cut the first joint of each chicken wing and discard wing tips. Holding small end of second joint, cut, scrape, and push meat down to thick end (see right). Pull skin and meat over end of bone with fingers to resemble baby drumsticks. Cut off knuckle end with scissors or knife. Repeat with remaining chicken wings.

THINK AHEAD
Make drummettes up to 2 days in advance. Cover and refrigerate.

COOKS' NOTE
The tips and first joint of chicken wings are basically just skin and bone. When making drummettes, reserve these parts for later use. They are ideal for making chicken stock.

HONEY MUSTARD CHICKEN DRUMMETTES

MAKES 20
8 garlic cloves, crushed
2 tbsp honey
2 tbsp Dijon mustard
2 tbsp light soy sauce
2 tbsp lemon juice
4 tbsp olive oil
2 tsp salt
1 tsp black pepper
1 recipe chicken drummettes (see above)

Combine garlic, honey, mustard, soy sauce, lemon, oil, salt, and pepper in a nonmetallic bowl. Add chicken and toss to coat each piece well. Cover and refrigerate for at least 1 hour.
Preheat oven to 350°F.
Place chicken on a wire rack set over a sheet pan. Bake until chicken is well browned and cooked through, 35 minutes.
Serve warm or at room temperature, with or without dips.

THINK AHEAD
Marinate chicken up to 1 day in advance. Cover and refrigerate.

GINGER HOISIN CHICKEN DRUMMETTES

MAKES 20
4-inch piece fresh ginger, grated
2 garlic cloves, crushed
6 tbsp hoisin sauce
1 tbsp Chinese hot chili sauce
1 tbsp light soy sauce
1 tbsp sugar
1 tbsp water
1 recipe chicken drummettes (see above)

Combine ginger, garlic, sauces, sugar, and water in a nonmetallic bowl.
Add chicken and toss to coat each piece well. Cover and refrigerate for at least 1 hour.
Preheat oven to 350°F.
Place chicken on a wire rack set over a sheet pan. Bake until chicken is well browned and cooked through, 35 minutes.
Serve warm or at room temperature, with or without dips.

THINK AHEAD
Marinate chicken up to 1 day in advance. Cover and refrigerate.

HONEY SESAME GLAZED COCKTAIL SAUSAGES

MAKES ABOUT 30
1lb cocktail sausages, separated
1 tbsp sesame seeds
½ tbsp honey

Preheat oven to 350°F. Arrange the sausages in a single layer on an oiled sheet pan. Bake for 20 minutes, then turn sausages over on the tray. Roast until golden and cooked through, 15 minutes. Sprinkle with sesame seeds and drizzle with honey. Toss to coat each sausage well. Serve hot or warm, with or without dips.

THINK AHEAD
Cook sausages up to 12 hours in advance. Cool and cover with foil. Reheat in 400°F oven, 10 minutes. Alternatively, cook sausages up to 1 hour in advance. Cover with foil and keep warm. Toss with seeds and honey just before serving.

COOKS' NOTE
If you can't find good quality cocktail sausages, use your favorite link sausages and cut into bite-sized pieces.

COCKTAIL SAUSAGE VARIATIONS

HONEY ROSEMARY GLAZED COCKTAIL SAUSAGES

Replace sesame seeds with 2 tsp finely chopped rosemary leaves.

SWEET AND SPICY GLAZED COCKTAIL SAUSAGES

Replace honey and sesame seeds with 1½ tbsp mango chutney.

CURRY SPICED YOGURT, CORIANDER, AND MANGO CHUTNEY DIP

MAKES ABOUT 2 CUPS

6 tbsp mango chutney
1 cup cilantro leaves, chopped
4 scallions, chopped juice of 2 limes
3/4 cup cream cheese
1 cup whole milk yogurt
½ tsp curry powder
¼ tsp turmeric
salt, tabasco

Place chutney, cilantro, scallions, lime, cream cheese, yogurt, and spices in a food processor or blender; pulse until well blended. Add salt and tabasco to taste. Cover and refrigerate for 30 minutes to allow the flavors to blend. Serve chilled with dippers.

THINK AHEAD
Make dip up to 1 day in advance. Cover and refrigerate.

COOKS' NOTE
Make this creamy yogurt dip Thai-style: omit the curry powder and replace the mango chutney with the same amount of Thai sweet chili sauce.

SALSA ROMESCO DIP

MAKES ABOUT 2 CUPS

1 red pepper, quartered and seeded
1 tbsp olive oil
½ cup blanched almonds
2-inch-thick slice of day-old bread, cubed
2 garlic cloves, chopped
¼ tsp cayenne pepper
½ tsp paprika
1 cup parsley leaves, chopped
2 tomatoes, chopped
2 tbsp sherry vinegar
salt, black pepper

Grill and peel pepper quarters (see page 147). Heat oil in pan over medium heat. Stir-fry almonds and bread cubes until golden, 5 minutes. Drain on paper towels. Place peeled pepper quarters, almonds, bread, garlic, spices, parsley, tomatoes, and vinegar in a food processor or blender; pulse until well blended but still retaining some texture. If necessary, adjust the consistency by gradually adding water 1 tbsp at a time. Add salt and pepper to taste. Cover and refrigerate for 30 minutes to allow the flavors to blend. Serve chilled with dippers.

THINK AHEAD
Make dip up to 3 days in advance. Cover and refrigerate.

COOKS' NOTES
You don't have to restrict yourself to using almonds in this piquant Catalan sauce. You can use hazelnuts, pine nuts, or a combination of either with the almonds, for equal authenticity.

ROAST RED PEPPER, FETA AND MINT DIP

MAKES ABOUT 2 CUPS

3 red peppers, quartered and seeded
1⅓ cups feta cheese
1 - 8oz package cream cheese
1 garlic clove, chopped
3 tbsp finely chopped fresh mint leaves
2 tbsp olive oil
1 tbsp lemon juice
salt, black pepper

Grill and peel pepper quarters (see page 147). Place peeled pepper quarters, feta and cream cheese, garlic, mint, oil, and lemon juice in a food processor or blender; pulse until well blended but still retaining some texture. If necessary, adjust consistency by gradually adding water 1 tbsp at a time. Add salt and pepper to taste. Cover and refrigerate for 30 minutes to allow the flavors to blend. Serve chilled with dippers.

THINK AHEAD
Make dip up to 3 days in advance. Cover and refrigerate.

AVOCADO LIME CREAM DIP

MAKES ABOUT 2 CUPS

2 medium avocados, peeled and pitted
4 scallions, chopped
2 green chilies, seeded and finely chopped
1 cup cilantro leaves
juice of 2 limes
1 tbsp olive oil
⅔ cup sour cream
salt

Place avocado, scallions, chilies, cilantro, lime, olive oil, and sour cream in a food processor or blender; pulse until smooth. Add salt to taste. Cover and refrigerate for 15 minutes to allow the flavors to blend. Serve chilled with dippers.

THINK AHEAD
Make dip up to 8 hours ahead. Cover and refrigerate.

COOKS' NOTE
To prevent the avocado cream dip from discoloring, make sure you press a piece of plastic wrap directly onto the surface of the dip. It's the oxygen in the air that turns avocado brown, so the less air that comes into contact with the dip, the better.

SUN-DRIED TOMATO AND CANNELLINI BEAN DIP

MAKES ABOUT 2 CUPS

2¾ cups canned cannellini beans, drained
8 sun-dried tomatoes in oil, drained
1 garlic clove, chopped
1 tbsp chopped rosemary leaves
4 tbsp olive oil
2 tbsp red wine vinegar
½ cup water
salt, black pepper

Place beans, sun-dried tomatoes, garlic, rosemary, oil, vinegar, and water in a food processor or blender; pulse to a smooth purée. If necessary, adjust the consistency by gradually adding more water, 1 tbsp at a time. Add salt and pepper to taste. Cover and refrigerate for 30 minutes to allow the flavors to blend. Serve chilled.

THINK AHEAD
Make dip up to 3 days in advance. Cover and refrigerate.

COOKS' NOTE
Cannellini are slender, ivory white Italian beans. Their creamy texture and their ability to absorb strong, aromatic flavors makes them ideal for dips. If you cannot find a source for cannellini beans, any canned white bean will make an excellent substitute.

HERBED YOGURT DIP

MAKES ABOUT 2 CUPS

1 cup parsley leaves, chopped
1 cup basil leaves, chopped
⅓ cup chives, chopped
grated zest of ½ lemon
juice of 1 lemon
1 - 8oz package cream cheese
1 cup whole milk yogurt
3 tbsp olive oil
salt, black pepper

Place herbs, lemon juice and zest, cream cheese, yogurt, and oil in a food processor or blender; pulse until well blended. Add salt and pepper to taste. Cover and refrigerate for 30 minutes to allow the flavors to blend. Serve chilled.

THINK AHEAD
Make dip up to 1 day in advance. Cover and refrigerate.

COOKS' NOTE
Use your favorite bouquet of green herbs to flavor this fragrant dip. Choose from arugula, tarragon, marjoram, chervil, or watercress instead of one or all of our favorite combination of parsley, basil and chives.
For a lighter dip, use ricotta cheese in place of some or all of the cream cheese.

CREAMY BLUE CHEESE AND SCALLION DIP

MAKES ABOUT 2 CUPS

6 scallions, chopped
1½ cups crumbled blue cheese
 (see cooks' note)
1¼ cups sour cream
1 tsp Worcestershire sauce
salt, black pepper

Place scallions, cheese, sour cream, and Worcestershire sauce in a food processor or blender; pulse until well blended but still retaining some texture. If necessary, adjust consistency by gradually adding water 1 tbsp at a time. Add salt and pepper to taste. Cover and refrigerate for 30 minutes to allow the flavors to blend. Serve chilled.

THINK AHEAD
Make dip up to 1 day in advance. Cover and refrigerate. Let stand at room temperature for 15 minutes to soften slightly before serving.

COOKS' NOTE
Your choice of blue cheese will determine the richness and piquancy of this delicious dip. Use Roquefort, Gorgonzola, or Stilton to intensify its zesty, pungent flavor. Try Danish blue to make a dip with a milder, mellower taste.

SPICY PEANUT DIP

MAKES ABOUT 2 CUPS

1 cup peanut butter
2 garlic cloves, crushed
1-inch piece fresh ginger, grated
juice of 1 lemon
4 tbsp soy sauce
2 tbsp honey
1 tsp turmeric
1 tsp tabasco
½ cup water
salt, black pepper

Place peanut butter, garlic, ginger, lemon, soy sauce, honey, turmeric, tabasco, and water in a food processor or blender; pulse until smooth. If necessary, adjust consistency by gradually adding extra water 1 tbsp at a time. Add salt and pepper to taste. Cover and refrigerate for 30 minutes to allow the flavors to blend. Serve chilled.

THINK AHEAD
Make dip up to 3 days in advance. Cover and refrigerate.

SPICED ROAST EGGPLANT DIP

MAKES ABOUT 2 CUPS

2 medium eggplants, pierced with fork
1 garlic clove, crushed
4 tbsp tahini
½ tsp ground cumin
1 tbsp lemon juice
½ cup whole-milk yogurt
salt, cayenne pepper

Preheat oven to 400°F.
Place eggplant on a baking pan and roast until skin is blistered and flesh feels soft, 45 minutes. When cool enough to handle, peel off charred skin and squeeze out as much moisture as possible from the flesh.
Place eggplant and garlic in a food processor or blender; pulse until smooth. Add tahini, cumin, lemon, and yogurt; pulse to a smooth purée. Add salt and cayenne pepper to taste. Cover and refrigerate for 30 minutes to allow the flavors to blend. Serve chilled with dippers.

THINK AHEAD
Make dip up to 3 days in advance. Cover and refrigerate.

COOKS' NOTE
For an extra smoky flavor, broil the eggplant directly over an open flame (either a barbecue or gas burner) until blackened on all sides. Peel and squeeze as directed.

TOPS AND BOTTOMS

TINY PARMESAN SHORTBREADS

MAKES 40

½ cup all-purpose flour, sifted
salt, cayenne pepper
3 tbsp cold butter, diced
¾ cup grated Parmesan cheese

ESSENTIAL EQUIPMENT
1½ -inch fluted pastry cutter, baking parchment

Preheat oven to 350°F.
Place flour, a pinch each salt and cayenne, butter, Parmesan, and any additional flavoring, if using, in a food processor; pulse to form a smooth dough. Roll out dough on a floured surface to a ¼-inch thickness. Stamp out 40 rounds with the pastry cutter. Place dough rounds on parchment-lined baking sheets ¾ inch apart and refrigerate for 30 minutes. Bake until golden brown, 8 minutes. Cool completely on a wire rack before topping.

THINK AHEAD
Bake shortbreads up to 2 weeks in advance. Store in an airtight container. Alternatively, bake and freeze up to 1 month in advance. Defrost and crisp in preheated 400°F oven for 3 minutes.

FLAVORED VARIATIONS

PARMESAN AND ROSEMARY SHORTBREADS

Add 1 tsp dried rosemary to the ingredients.

PARMESAN AND BLACK OLIVE SHORTBREADS

Add 1 tsp finely chopped black olives to the ingredients.

TINY PARMESAN AND ROSEMARY SHORTBREADS WITH ROAST CHERRY TOMATOES AND FETA

MAKES 40

20 cherry tomatoes, halved
2 tsp olive oil
½ tsp honey
salt, black pepper
1 cup crumbled feta cheese
10 pitted black olives, quartered
Rosemary leves to garnish
1 recipe tiny Parmesan and rosemary shortbreads (see left)

Preheat oven 400°F. Place tomato halves on an sheet pan and sprinkle with oil, honey, salt, and pepper. Roast in oven until softened, 20 minutes. Top shortbreads with tomatoes and feta. Garnish with olives and rosemary leaves. Serve at room temperature.

THINK AHEAD
Prepare tomatoes up to 1 day in advance. Cover and refrigerate. Bring to room temperature before using. Top shortbreads up to 2 hours before serving.

TINY PARMESAN AND BLACK OLIVE SHORTBREADS WITH PARSLEY PESTO AND GOAT'S CHEESE

MAKES 40

1 cup parsley leaves
2 tbsp pine nuts
4 tbsp grated Parmesan cheese
1 garlic clove, crushed
1 tbsp olive oil
salt, black pepper
½ cup fresh creamy goat cheese
1 recipe tiny Parmesan and black olive shortbreads (see far left)

Place parsley, pine nuts, Parmesan, garlic, and oil in a food processor or blender; pulse to a thick paste. Add salt and pepper to taste. Use a teaspoon to top shortbreads with pesto and goat cheese. Serve at room temperature.

THINK AHEAD
Make pesto up to 3 days in advance. Top shortbreads up to 2 hours before serving.

COCKTAIL CORN CAKES WITH SPICY MANGO SALSA

MAKES 20

FOR PANCAKES	FOR SALSA
3 tbsp medium-ground cornmeal	½ mango, finely diced (see page 163)
½ cup all-purpose flour	½ medium red onion, finely chopped
¼ tsp salt	
¼ tsp baking powder	1 fresh green chili, seeded and finely diced
1 egg, beaten	
5 tbsp milk	juice of 1 lime
1 tbsp melted butter	salt, black pepper
¾ cup corn kernels	½ cup crème fraîche or sour cream
cayenne pepper	
1 tbsp sunflower oil	20 fresh cilantro leaves

Mix the cornmeal, flour, salt, baking powder, egg, milk, and butter to make a smooth batter. Stir in corn kernels. Add cayenne pepper to taste.

Brush a frying pan or griddle with oil. Preheat over medium heat. Working in batches, drop heaped teaspoonfuls of mixture into the hot pan. Cook until crisp and golden, 2½ minutes per side. Brush pan with more oil between each batch of pancakes. Cool pancakes to room temperature.

For salsa, combine mango, onion, chili, and lime. Add salt and pepper to taste. Top each cake with 1 teaspoonful each crème fraîche or sour cream and salsa. Garnish with cilantro leaves. Serve at room temperature.

THINK AHEAD
Make cakes up to 1 day in advance. Store in an airtight container in the refrigerator. Crisp in preheated 400°F oven for 3 minutes. Make salsa up to 5 hours in advance. Cover and refrigerate. Top pancakes 45 minutes before serving.

COOKS' NOTE
The best flavor comes from fresh corn. Scrape kernels off the cob with a sharp knife. Use canned corn, drained, frozen corn, defrosted, when fresh is not available.

WILD RICE AND SCALLION PANCAKES WITH AVOCADO LIME SALSA

MAKES 20

FOR PANCAKES	FOR SALSA
4 tbsp wild rice	1 small avocado, peeled, pitted and finely diced
2 tbsp basmati rice	
½ cup all-purpose flour	½ medium red onion, finely chopped
¼ tsp salt	
1 egg, beaten	juice of 1 lime
4 tbsp milk	1 tbsp olive oil
2 tbsp finely chopped scallion	salt, tabasco
1 tbsp sunflower oil	2 scallions, white stems only

Cook each type of rice in a separate pot of boiling water until tender; wild rice, for 40 minutes, basmati rice, for 12 minutes. Drain and cool. Mix the flour, salt, egg, and milk together to make a smooth batter. Stir both types of cooked rice and the chopped scallions into the batter.

Brush a frying pan or griddle with oil. Preheat over medium heat. Working in batches, drop heaped teaspoonfuls of mixture into the hot pan. Cook until crisp and golden, 2½ minutes per side. Brush pan with more oil between each batch of pancakes. Cool pancakes to room temperature.

For salsa, combine avocado, onion, lime, and oil. Add salt and tabasco to taste. For garnish, cut scallions into 1½-inch pieces. Cut each piece into quarters lengthwise. Top pancakes with equal amounts of salsa. Garnish each pancake a slice of scallion. Serve at room temperature.

THINK AHEAD
Make pancakes up to 1 day in advance. Store in an airtight container in the refrigerator. Crisp in preheated 400°F oven, 3 minutes. Make salsa up to 2 hours in advance. Cover and refrigerate. Top pancakes 45 minutes before serving.

HERB PANCAKES

MAKES 20

½ cup all-purpose flour
¼ tsp baking powder
¼ tsp salt
1 egg, beaten
3 tbsp milk
1 tbsp finely chopped fresh herbs
1 tbsp sunflower oil

Sift flour, baking powder, and salt together. Make a well in the center. Add egg and milk to well. Gradually stir in flour and mix to a smooth batter. Stir in herbs (see below). Brush a frying pan or griddle with oil. Preheat over medium heat. Working in batches, drop heaped teaspoonfuls of mixture into the hot pan. Cook until bubbles appear and underside is golden, 3 minutes. Turn and brown other side, 2 minutes. Brush pan with more oil between each batch of pancakes. Cool pancakes. Serve at room temperature.

THINK AHEAD
Make pancakes up to 2 days in advance. Store in an airtight container in the refrigerator. Crisp in preheated 400°F oven for 3 minutes.

VARIATIONS

DILL PANCAKES

Add 1 tbsp finely chopped dill to the ingredients.

CHIVE PANCAKES

Add 1 tbsp finely chopped chives to the ingredients.

DILL PANCAKES WITH SALMON CAVIAR AND LEMON CREME FRAICHE

MAKES 20

1 tsp grated lemon zest
1 tbsp lemon juice
½ cup crème fraîche or sour cream
1 recipe dill pancakes (see above)
6 tbsp salmon caviar
20 dill sprigs to garnish

Mix lemon zest and juice into crème fraîche. Top each pancake with 1 teaspoonful each crème fraîche or sour cream and salmon caviar. Garnish with dill. Serve at room temperature.

THINK AHEAD
Make lemon crème fraîche up to 1 day in advance. Cover and refrigerate. Top pancakes up to 45 minutes before serving.

CHIVE PANCAKES WITH CREME FRAICHE AND RED ONION CONFIT

MAKES 20

2 tbsp sugar
1 tbsp water
1 tbsp red wine vinegar
1 medium red onion, finely sliced
salt, black pepper
1 recipe chive pancakes (see left)
½ cup crème fraîche or sour cream
1 tbsp finely chopped fresh chives

Put sugar and water in a small pan and stir to dissolve. Bring to a boil over medium-low heat and cook to a dark caramel (see page 145). Remove from heat and add vinegar and onions. Return to medium heat and stir fry until onions soften, 5 minutes. Add salt and pepper to taste. Cool to warm. Top each pancake with 1 teaspoonful each crème fraîche or sour cream and onions. Garnish with chives. Serve at room temperature.

THINK AHEAD
Make onion confit up to 1 day in advance. Cover and store at room temperature. Top pancakes up to 45 minutes before serving.

BUCKWHEAT BLINIS WITH SOUR CREAM AND CAVIAR

MAKES 20

1 cup buckwheat flour
¼ tsp baking powder
¼ tsp salt
1 egg, separated
¾ cup milk
½ cup sour cream
½ cup caviar

Sift flour, baking powder, and salt together. Make a well in the center of the flour. Beat egg yolk and milk. Add to the well. Gradually stir flour into the egg mixture. Mix to a smooth batter. Beat egg white until it holds soft peaks (see page 141). Gently fold the beaten egg white into the batter. Brush a frying pan or griddle with oil. Preheat over medium heat. Working in batches, drop heaped teaspoonfuls of mixture into the hot pan. Cook until bubbles appear and underside is golden, 3 minutes. Turn and brown other side, 2 minutes. Brush pan with oil between each batch of blinis. Cool blinis before topping. Top each blini with 1 teaspoonful each sour cream and caviar. Serve at room temperature.

THINK AHEAD
Make blinis up to 2 days in advance. Store in airtight container in refrigerator. Crisp in preheated 400°F oven, 3 minutes. Top up to 30 minutes before serving.

CROSTINI

MAKES 20

20 - ½-inch-thick slices day-old baguette
4 tbsp olive oil

Preheat oven 350°F. Place baguette slices on a baking sheet. Brush with olive oil. Bake until crisp and lightly golden, 10 minutes. Serve plain or topped according to the following recipes.

THINK AHEAD
Make crostini up to 2 weeks in advance. Cool completely and store in an airtight container at room temperature.

COOKS' NOTE
Choose a thin baguette about 2–3 inches in diameter. Add a crushed clove of garlic to the oil before brushing the bread for extra flavor.

SPICY SHRIMP CROSTINI

MAKES 20

½ lb precooked baby shrimp
½ medium red onion, finely chopped
1 garlic clove, crushed
½ tsp crushed red pepper flakes
2 tbsp olive oil
1 tbsp lemon juice
salt, black pepper
1 tbsp finely chopped parsley leaves
1 recipe crostini (see left)

Combine shrimp with onion, garlic, red pepper flakes oil, and lemon. Add salt and pepper to taste and stir in parsley. Spoon on to crostini. Serve at room temperature.

THINK AHEAD
Make topping up to 1 day in advance, but add salt, pepper, and parsley just before serving for the best texture and color. Store in an airtight container in the refrigerator. Top crostini up to 1 hour before serving.

TOMATO AND BASIL CROSTINI

MAKES 20

5 ripe plum tomatoes, seeded and diced
  (see page 147)
½ medium red onion, finely chopped
1 garlic clove, crushed
2 tbsp olive oil
1 tbsp balsamic vinegar
salt, black pepper
1 recipe crostini (see far left)
20 tiny basil leaves to garnish

Mix tomato, onion, garlic, oil, and vinegar together. Add salt and pepper to taste. Spoon onto crostini. Garnish with basil leaves. Serve at room temperature.

THINK AHEAD
Make topping up to 1 day in advance, but add the salt and pepper just before serving. Store in an airtight container in the refrigerator. Top crostini up to 45 minutes before serving.

COOKS' NOTE
Basil is the tomato's classic culinary partner. Try arugula in place of basil for a deep, peppery bite. Stir in a handful of sliced arugula just before serving. Reserve some smaller leaves for the garnish.

WHITE BEAN AND SAGE CROSTINI

MAKES 20
3 tbsp olive oil
1 small onion, finely chopped
2 garlic cloves, finely minced
4 sage leaves, finely chopped
2 ¾ cups canned cannellini beans, drained
2 tbsp water
salt, black pepper
1 recipe crostini (see page 42)
1 seeded ripe tomato, diced (see page 147)
extra olive oil for drizzling

Heat oil in a saucepan. Add onion, garlic, and sage and cook over a low heat until soft, about 5 minutes. Add beans, water, and salt and pepper to taste. Cook for about 10 minutes. Mash the beans with a wooden spoon to make a rough purée. Spread bean purée on crostini. Top each crostini with a little tomato dice and a drizzle of olive oil. Serve warm or at room temperature.

THINK AHEAD
Make topping up to 3 days in advance. Cover and refrigerate. Return to room temperature before serving. Top crostini up to 1 hour before serving.

AVOCADO AND GOAT CHEESE CROSTINI

MAKES 20
1 large avocado, peeled and pitted
¾ cup fresh creamy goat cheese
grated zest and juice of 1 lemon
1 tbsp olive oil
salt, tabasco
1 recipe crostini (see page 42)

Place avocado, cheese, zest, juice, and oil in a food processor or blender; pulse to a smooth purée. Add salt and tabasco to taste. Spoon topping onto each crostini. Serve at room temperature.

THINK AHEAD
Make topping up to 6 hours in advance. Store in a bowl with plastic wrap, pressing directly onto purée to prevent contact with air. This will prevent discoloration. Keep refrigerated and stir before using. Top crostini up to 20 minutes before serving.

EGGPLANT CAVIAR CROSTINI

MAKES 20
2 medium eggplants, pierced with a fork
1 garlic clove, crushed
juice of ½ lemon
2 tbsp olive oil
1 tbsp whole-milk yogurt
salt, cayenne pepper
1 recipe crostini (see page 42)
20 mint sprigs to garnish
1 tsp paprika to garnish

Broil eggplant until skin is black and blistered, and the flesh feels soft. When cool enough to handle, peel off charred skin. Use hands to squeeze out as much moisture as possible from the flesh. Place eggplant, garlic, lemon juice, oil, and yogurt in a food processor or blender; pulse to a smooth purée. Add salt and cayenne pepper to taste. Cool completely. Spoon topping onto each crostini. Garnish with mint sprigs and a pinch of paprika. Serve at room temperature.

THINK AHEAD
Make topping up to 2 days in advance. Cover and refrigerate. Top crostini up to 45 minutes before serving.

MINI CHERRY TOMATO AND BASIL PESTO GALETTES

MAKES 20

1 cup basil leaves
2 tbsp pine nuts
1 tbsp olive oil
4 tbsp grated Parmesan cheese
1 sheet puff pastry
20 cherry tomatoes, each cut into 3 slices
salt, black pepper
20 basil sprigs to garnish

ESSENTIAL EQUIPMENT
2-inch fluted pastry cutter

For pesto, place basil, pine nuts, oil, and Parmesan in a food processor or blender; pulse to a thick paste. Preheat oven to 400°F. Roll out pastry on a floured surface to a ⅛-inch thickness. Cut out 20 rounds with the pastry cutter. Follow scoring instructions as shown in far-left bottom illustrations. Place pastry rounds on a floured baking sheet. Spread ½ tsp pesto on each round and top with 3 cherry tomato slices. Sprinkle with salt and pepper. Bake until crisp and golden, 10 minutes. Garnish each galette with ½ tsp pesto and a basil sprig. Serve warm.

THINK AHEAD
Make pesto up to 3 days in advance. Cover and refrigerate. Bake galettes up to 1 day in advance. Reheat in a preheated 400°F oven for 3 minutes. Garnish and serve warm.

MINI MANGO GALETTES

MAKES 20

1 sheet package puff pastry
1¼ cups canned sliced mangoes or peaches
2 tbsp apricot jam
2 tsp powdered sugar for dusting

Preheat oven to 400°F.
Roll out pastry on a floured surface to a ⅛-inch thickness. Cut pastry into approximately 20 squares, measuring 2 x 2 inches each. Trace a fine line inside each square using a sharp knife (see below, left). Be careful not to actually cut through the pastry. Pierce the center of each square with a fork (see below, right). Place pastry squares on a floured baking sheet. Cut mango slices across into ¼-inch-thick slices. Arrange 2 or 3 mango pieces, slightly overlapping, on top of each pastry square. Bake until pastry is crisp and golden, 10 minutes. Melt apricot jam with 1 tbsp water over low heat to make glaze. Allow galettes to cool, then brush with apricot glaze. Dust with powdered sugar. Serve at room temperature.

THINK AHEAD
Same as mini apple galettes.

MAKING PASTRY SQUARES
Make up to 3 hours in advance.

Trace a fine line using a sharp knife.

Prick center with a fork.

MINI APPLE GALETTES

MAKES 20

1 sheet puff pastry
2 apples, quartered and cored
2 tbsp apricot jam
2 tsp powdered sugar for dusting

ESSENTIAL EQUIPMENT
2-inch plain pastry cutter

Preheat oven to 400°F. Roll out pastry on a floured surface to a ⅛-inch thickness. Cut out 20 rounds with the pastry cutter. Trace a fine line inside each round using a sharp knife (see below, far left). Be careful not to actually cut through the pastry. Pierce the center of each pastry round with a fork (see below, left). Place rounds onto a floured baking sheet.
Cut each apple quarter crosswise into fine slices. Arrange apple slices, slightly overlapping, on each pastry round. Bake until pastry is crisp and golden, 10 minutes. Melt apricot jam with 1 tbsp water over low heat to make glaze. Allow galettes to cool, then brush with apricot glaze. Dust with powdered sugar. Serve at room temperature.

THINK AHEAD
Assemble and bake up to 1 day in advance. Store in an airtight container at room temperature. Glaze up to 5 hours in advance.

ROAST RED ONION AND THYME FOCACCINE

MAKES 20

1 recipe unbaked bread dough
  (see page 140)
1¼ cups grated Gruyère cheese
1 medium red onion, quartered
coarse salt, black pepper
3 thyme sprigs, roughly chopped

ESSENTIAL EQUIPMENT
2-inch plain pastry cutter

Preheat oven to 400°F.
Roll out dough on a floured surface to a
¼-inch thickness. Cut out 20 rounds
with the pastry cutter. Place on a
floured baking sheet and sprinkle with
cheese. Cut each onion quarter across
into 5 slices. Place a slice on top of each
round. Sprinkle with salt, pepper, and
thyme. Bake until crisp and golden,
15 minutes. Serve warm.

THINK AHEAD
Bake up to 1 day in advance. Store in an airtight
container at room temperature. Crisp in a preheated
400°F oven for 10 minutes. Alternatively, assemble
and freeze unbaked for up to 1 month (see page
149). Bake frozen focaccine in preheated
400°F oven for 20 minutes.

POTATO AND ROSEMARY FOCACCINE

MAKES 20

20 small new potatoes
1 recipe unbaked bread dough
  (see page 140)
1¼ cups grated Gruyère cheese
½ tsp salt, ¼ tsp black pepper
3 rosemary sprigs, separated into 20 pieces
  (see page 147)

ESSENTIAL EQUIPMENT
2-inch plain pastry cutter

Preheat oven to 400°F. Cut potatoes into
¼-inch-thick slices. Place potato slices in
boiling water and cook for 5 minutes
from the time the water has returned to
a boil. Drain and cool. Roll out dough
on a floured surface to a ¼-inch
thickness. Cut out 20 rounds with the
pastry cutter. Place on a floured
baking sheet. Sprinkle all the rounds
evenly with about three quarters of the
cheese. Arrange 4 potato slices on top of
each round. Sprinkle with the remaining
cheese and salt and pepper. Top each
round with a tuft of rosemary. Bake until
crisp and golden, 15 minutes. Serve warm.

THINK AHEAD
Bake up to 1 day in advance. Store in an airtight
container at room temperature. Crisp in a preheated
400°F oven for 10 minutes. Alternatively, assemble
and freeze unbaked for up to 1 month (see page
149). Bake frozen focaccine in preheated 400°F
oven for 20 minutes.

ARTICHOKE AND GORGONZOLA FOCACCINE

MAKES 20

1 recipe unbaked bread dough
  (see page 140)
1 cup crumbled Gorgonzola or Danish
  blue cheese
salt, black pepper
20 baby artichokes hearts in oil, drained
  and halved
2 tbsp oregano leaves

ESSENTIAL EQUIPMENT
2-inch plain pastry cutter

Preheat oven to 400°F. Roll out dough
on a floured surface to a ¼-inch
thickness. Cut out 20 rounds with the
pastry cutter. Place onto a floured
baking sheet. Sprinkle each round with
cheese, salt and pepper. Top with
2 artichoke halves. Bake until crisp
and golden, 15 minutes. Garnish with
oregano leaves and serve warm.

THINK AHEAD
Bake up to 1 day in advance. Store in an airtight
container at room temperature. Crisp in a preheated
400°F oven for 10 minutes. Alternatively, assemble
and freeze unbaked for up to 1 month (see page
149). Bake frozen focaccine in preheated
400°F oven for 20 minutes.

CROUTES

MAKES 20

7 slices white bread

ESSENTIAL EQUIPMENT
2-inch fluted pastry cutter

Preheat oven to 300°F. With the pastry cutter, cut each slice into 3 rounds. Place on a baking sheet and bake until crisp, 25 minutes. Cool.

THINK AHEAD
Make up to 3 days in advance. Store in an airtight container at room temperature.

GRILLED BEEF FILLET WITH SALSA VERDE CROUTES

MAKES 20

1 cup parsley leaves
10 basil leaves
10 mint leaves
1 garlic clove, crushed
1 tbsp Dijon mustard
1 tbsp drained capers
2 drained anchovy fillets
2 tbsp olive oil
salt, black pepper
¾ lb beef fillet steak, sliced ¾-inch thick
1 recipe croutes (see above)

ESSENTIAL EQUIPMENT
1½-inch plain pastry cutter, cast-iron grill pan

For salsa, place fresh herbs, garlic, mustard, capers, anchovies, and oil in a food processor or blender; pulse to a thick paste. Add salt and pepper to taste. Stamp steak into 20 rounds with a pastry cutter (see below). Preheat grill pan over high heat. Sear steak rounds, about 3 minutes per side. Sprinkle with salt and pepper. Place one round on each croute. Top with salsa. Serve warm or at room temperature.

FRESH SALMON TARTARE CROUTES

MAKES 20

½ lb fresh salmon fillet
juice of 1 lemon
2 tbsp drained cornichons, finely chopped
2 tbsp drained capers, finely chopped
1 tbsp mayonnaise (see page 142)
1 tsp grainy mustard
1 tbsp finely chopped tarragon
½ tsp salt
½ tsp tabasco
½ lemon, peeled (see page 147)
1 recipe croutes (see above)

Cut salmon into fine dice and place in a nonreactive bowl. Toss salmon pieces with lemon juice to coat. Cover and refrigerate for 3 hours. Drain lemon juice and discard. Add cornichons, capers, mayonnaise, mustard, tarragon, and salt to salmon. Stir to coat. Add tabasco to taste. Cut lemon into segment wedges (see below). Spoon salmon tartare onto croutes. Garnish with lemon wedges. Served chilled.

THINK AHEAD
Prepare topping up to 1 day in advance. Cover and refrigerate. Top croutes up to 30 minutes in advance. Garnish and serve chilled.

CUTTING OUT STEAK ROUNDS

LEMON SEGMENTS
Cut lemon half into 4 slices.

Cut each slice into wedges.

GRIDDLED SCALLOPS WITH SWEET CHILI SAUCE AND CREME FRAICHE

MAKES 20

10 sea scallops
salt, black pepper
4 tbsp Thai sweet chili sauce
1 recipe croutes (see page 46)
6 tbsp crème fraîche or sour cream
20 cilantro leaves to garnish

ESSENTIAL EQUIPMENT
cast-iron grill pan

Cut each scallop in half horizonally. Preheat grill pan over high heat. Sear scallops, 1 minute per side. Sprinkle with salt and pepper to taste and toss with chili sauce. Place 1 scallop half on each croute. Top with 1 tsp crème fraîche. Garnish with cilantro leaves. Serve at room temperature or chilled.

THINK AHEAD
Sear and sauce scallops up to 1 day in advance. Cover and refrigerate. Top croutes up to 1 hour in advance.

COOKS' NOTE
For an even better flavor, grill the scallops 3 inches above medium hot coals. Cook for 1 minute per side.

SEARED TUNA NICOISE CROUTES

MAKES 20

7oz tuna steak, sliced 1-inch thick
salt, black pepper
½ romaine heart, leaves separated
10 green beans
1 tomato, seeded and diced (see page 147)
2 tbsp drained baby capers
10 anchovy fillets, roughly chopped
10 pitted black olives, sliced
2 tbsp olive oil
1 tbsp red wine vinegar
salt, black pepper
1 recipe croutes (see page 46)
2 tbsp mayonnaise (see page 142)

ESSENTIAL EQUIPMENT
cast-iron grill pan.

Cut tuna into 1-inch cubes. Preheat grill pan over high heat. Sear tuna cubes on both sides until firm to the touch, 2 minutes per side. Season with salt and pepper. Cool. Cut stalks from salad leaves and discard. Cut each leaf into 1-inch pieces. Cut beans into ½-inch lengths. Put beans in to a pan of boiling water. Once the water returns to a boil, drain beans and refresh in cold water. Pat dry with paper towels. Toss beans, tomato, capers, anchovies, and olives with oil and vinegar. Add salt and pepper to taste. Spread each croute with mayonnaise and top with a salad leaf. Place tuna on top. Garnish with vegetables. Serve at room temperature.

THINK AHEAD
Prepare vegetables up to 1 day in advance. Cover and refrigerate. Cook tuna up to 2 hours in advance. Keep at room temperature until ready to assemble. Top croutes up to 1 hour in advance.

ASPARAGUS CROUTES WITH LEMON HOLLANDAISE

MAKES 20

10 medium asparagus tips, halved lengthwise
1 small bunch chives
1 recipe lemon hollandaise (see page 143)
1 recipe croutes (see page 46)
1 tsp paprika to dust

Put asparagus in a pan of boiling water. Once the water returns to a boil, drain asparagus and refresh immediately in cold water. Pat dry with paper towel. Cut chives on the diagonal into 1-inch lengths. Spoon hollandaise onto croutes and top with asparagus halves. Dust with paprika. Garnish with chives. Serve at room temperature.

THINK AHEAD
Cook asparagus up to 1 day in advance. Cover and refrigerate. Top croutes up to 1 hour in advance.

TINY SCONES

MAKES 10

¾ cup all-purpose flour
1½ tsp baking powder
pinch of salt
3 tbsp butter, diced
1½ tbsp sugar
1 egg, beaten
¼ cup cream

ESSENTIAL EQUIPMENT
1½-inch fluted pastry cutter
Preheat oven to 400°F.

Sift flour, baking powder, and salt. Crumble the butter into the flour with fingers until mixture resembles fine crumbs. Stir in sugar (omit if making savory scones) and any additional flavoring, if using. With a fork, stir in egg and enough cream to make a soft dough. Turn dough onto a floured surface; knead lightly until smooth. Sprinkle surface with more flour and gently roll out to a 1-inch thickness. Stamp out 10 rounds with pastry cutter. Place rounds on a greased and floured baking sheet. Bake until firm and golden, 8–10 minutes. Cool on a wire rack.

VARIATIONS

TINY DILL SCONES

Replace sugar with 1 tbsp finely chopped dill.

TINY HEART-SHAPED SCONES

Stamp out dough with a 2½-inch heart-shaped pastry cutter.

THINK AHEAD
Bake scones up to 1 week in advance. Store in an airtight container at room temperature.

COOKS' NOTE
Cover the scones with a cloth as they cool on the wire rack. This will keep some of the steam in, making the scones perfectly soft, moist, and light.

TINY DILL SCONES WITH SMOKED TROUT AND HORSERADISH CREAM

MAKES 20

1 recipe tiny dill scones (see above)
½ cup sour cream
1 tbsp horseradish sauce
5oz smoked trout or salmon slices
black pepper
20 tiny dill sprigs to garnish

Cut each scone in half. Combine cream and horseradish sauce. Top each scone half with an equal amount of mixture. Cut smoked trout slices into 20 1-inch-wide strips. Top each scone with a smoked trout strip and a sprinkle of pepper. Garnish with dill sprigs. Serve at room temperature.

THINK AHEAD
Top scones up to 45 minutes in advance. Garnish just before serving.

TINY CREAM TEA SCONES WITH RASPBERRY PRESERVES

MAKES 20

1 recipe tiny scones (see top of page)
⅓ cup raspberry preserves
½ cup heavy cream

Cut each scone in half. Whip cream until it holds soft peaks (see page 144). Top each scone half with 1 tsp each preserves and cream. Serve at room temperature.

THINK AHEAD
Top scones up to 30 minutes in advance.

TINY HEART SHORTCAKES WITH STRAWBERRIES

MAKES 20

1 recipe heart-shaped tiny scones (see top of page)
½ cup heavy cream
2 tbsp sugar
10 strawberries, hulled and halved
2 tsp powdered sugar for dusting

ESSENTIAL EQUIPMENT
Piping bag with a large star tip

Cut each scone in half. Whip cream until it holds stiff peaks. Beat in sugar (see page 144). Fill piping bag with cream. Pipe 3 small rosettes on each scone half (see page 146). Arrange strawberry on top. Dust with powdered sugar. Serve at room temperature.

THINK AHEAD
Top scones up to 30 minutes in advance.

MINI PISSALADIERE

MAKES 24

1 recipe unbaked short-crust pastry
  (see page 136)
1 tbsp olive oil
1 garlic clove, crushed
2 large spanish onions, finely sliced
¾ cup tomato puree
1 tsp dried oregano
salt, black pepper
1 tbsp grated Parmesan cheese
24 pitted black olives
6 anchovies, halved lengthwise

ESSENTIAL EQUIPMENT
14 x 10-inch jelly-roll pan

Preheat oven to 400°F.
Grease jelly-roll pan. Roll out pastry on
a floured surface to fit pan. Place pastry
in an oiled pan. Heat olive oil in a frying
pan over medium heat. Add garlic and
onion and cook until soft, 10 minutes.
Add tomato puree and continue cooking
for 5 minutes. Add oregano, and salt and
pepper to taste. Spread onion mixture
evenly over pastry. Bake for 15 minutes.
Remove from oven and sprinkle with
Parmesan. Allow to cool in pan then cut
into 24 squares, 2 x 2 inches each.
Cut anchovy pieces in half crosswise.
Top each square with 2 anchovy pieces
in a crisscross pattern with an olive in
the center. Remove from pan and serve
at room temperature.

THINK AHEAD
Make, cut and garnish, but leave in pan, up to
2 days in advance. Store in pan covered in the
refrigerator. Crisp in preheated 400°F oven for
10 minutes. Remove from pan before serving.

EGGPLANT AND PINE NUT PIZZETTE

MAKES 20

1 recipe unbaked bread dough
  (see page 140)
1 medium eggplant
1 tbsp olive oil
1 garlic clove, crushed
2 tbsp finely chopped parsley leaves
½ cup tomato puree
4 tbsp grated Parmesan cheese
3 tbsp pine nuts
salt, black pepper

ESSENTIAL EQUIPMENT
2-inch plain pastry cutter

Preheat oven to 400°F
Roll out dough on a floured surface to
a ⅛-inch thickness. Cut out 20 rounds
with the pastry cutter and place on a
floured baking sheet.
Cut eggplant in half lengthwise, then cut
halves into ¼-inch-thick slices. Heat oil
in a frying pan and add eggplant, garlic,
and parsley. Stir fry over high heat until
wilted, 5 minutes.
Spread each pizzette with 1 tsp tomato
puree. Arrange eggplant slices on top.
Sprinkle with Parmesan, pine nuts, salt
and pepper. Bake until crisp and golden,
10 minutes. Serve warm.

THINK AHEAD
Make up to 1 day in advance. Cover and refrigerate.
Crisp in preheated 400°F oven for 10 minutes
before serving.

TOMATO AND BASIL PIZZETTE

MAKES 20

1 recipe unbaked bread dough
  (see page 140)
½ cup tomato puree
1 cup small basil leaves
4oz mozzarella cheese, finely sliced
4 tbsp grated Parmesan cheese
salt, black pepper

ESSENTIAL EQUIPMENT
2-inch plain pastry cutter

Preheat oven to 400°F.
Roll dough out on a floured surface to
a ⅛-inch thickness. Cut out 20 rounds
with the pastry cutter and place on a
floured baking sheet.
Cut mozzarella slices into 20 equal-sized
pieces. Spread each round with 1 tsp
tomato puree and top with 2 basil
leaves. Place a piece of mozzarella on
top. Sprinkle with Parmesan, salt, and
pepper. Bake until crisp and golden,
10 minutes. Serve warm.

THINK AHEAD
Make up to 1 day in advance. Cover and refrigerate.
Crisp in preheated 400°F oven for 10 minutes
before serving.

MINI APPLE TATINS

MAKES 20

1 sheet puff pastry
½ cup sugar
2 tbsp water
2½ apples, peeled, cored, and quartered
2 tsp powdered sugar for dusting

ESSENTIAL EQUIPMENT
2 - 12 cup mini muffin pans, 2-inch plain
pastry cutter

Preheat oven 400°F.
Roll out pastry on a floured surface to a ¼-inch thickness.
Cut out 20 rounds with the pastry cutter.
Put sugar and water in a small pan. Stir to dissolve, then place over medium heat and bring to a boil. Cook to a dark caramel (see page 145). Divide caramel evenly among 20 of the muffin pans.
Cut each apple quarter crosswise into 6 slices, about ¼-inch thick. Arrange 3 apple pieces over the caramel in each cup. Press pastry rounds on top. Bake until pastry is crisp and golden, 10 minutes. Cool slightly before inverting onto a rack. Dust with powered sugar. Serve warm.

THINK AHEAD
Bake up to 1 day in advance, but do not turn out of pans. Store covered at room temperature. Reheat in preheated 400°F oven for 10 minutes. Finish as directed.

COOKS' NOTE
In France, Golden Delicious apples are traditionally used for making tarte tatin. This is because they retain their shape well and do not disintegrate when baked. Granny Smith apples, however, also give good results.

MINI RED ONION TATINS

MAKES 20

2 red onions, quartered
2 tsp finely chopped thyme leaves
salt, black pepper
1 tbsp olive oil
1 sheet puff pastry
½ cup sugar
2 tbsp water
1 tbsp balsamic vinegar
3 thyme sprigs, roughly chopped, to garnish

ESSENTIAL EQUIPMENT
2 - 12-cup mini muffin pans, 2-inch plain pastry cutter

Preheat oven to 400°F. Cut each onion quarter crosswise into 5 pieces, about ¼ inch thick each. Place pieces on an greased baking sheet. Sprinkle with chopped thyme, salt, pepper, and oil. Bake for 10 minutes. Meanwhile, roll out pastry on a floured surface to a ¼-inch thickness. Cut out 20 rounds with the pastry cutter. Put sugar and water in a small pan and stir to dissolve. Place over medium heat and bring to a boil. Cook to a dark caramel (see page 145). Divide caramel evenly among 20 of the muffin cups. Arrange 2 onion pieces over the caramel in each muffin cup. Press pastry rounds on top. Bake until pastry is crisp and golden, 10 minutes. Cool slightly before inverting. Sprinkle with thyme and drizzle with vinegar. Serve warm.

THINK AHEAD
Bake up to 1 day in advance, but do not turn out of tins. Store covered at room temperature. Reheat in preheated 400°F oven for 5 minutes.
Invert onto a platter or rack and finish as directed.

CANAPES

MAKES 20

7 thin slices bread

SPECIAL EQUIPMENT
2-inch fluted pastry cutter

Cut bread slices into 20 rounds with
the pastry cutter.

THINK AHEAD
Prepare up to 1 day in advance. Store in an
airtight container.

COOKS' NOTE
We urge you to look beyond white and whole-
wheat bread for canapé bases; the wealth of
speciality breads now available offers a shortcut
to simple but flavorsome canapés. Also try using
different shaped cutters—another easy but
surefire way to add instant appeal.

GRAVLAX PUMPERNICKEL CANAPES WITH DILL-MUSTARD SAUCE

MAKES 20

1½ tsp white wine vinegar

2 tsp sugar

2 tbsp Dijon mustard

1 tbsp finely chopped dill

1 tsp white pepper

2½ tbsp sunflower oil

5 pumpernickel slices

10oz gravlax slices

chopped dill for garnish

For sauce, combine vinegar, sugar,
mustard, dill, and pepper; whisk in oil
until thick and creamy. Lay gravlax on
the pumpernickel slices. Cut each
pumpernickel and gravlax slice into
20 - 1-inch-wide strips. Drizzle with
sauce. Garnish with additional dill.
Serve chilled or at room temperature.

THINK AHEAD
Assemble up to 3 hours in advance. Cover tightly
with plastic wrap and refrigerate. Drizzle with sauce
up to 1 hour before serving.

VALENTINE CUCUMBER CREAM CANAPES

MAKES 20

½ cucumber

1 - 8oz package cream cheese

10 thin white bread slices

3 tbsp finely chopped parsley leaves

salt, white pepper

ESSENTIAL EQUIPMENT
1½ -inch heart-shaped pastry cutter
2½ -inch heart-shaped pastry cutter

Cut cucumber into ¼ -inch slices.
With smaller cutter, cut out 20 cucumber
hearts. Spread cream cheese on bread.
Cut out 20 canapé hearts with larger
pastry cutter. Put parsley on small dish.
Dip edges of canapés in parsley. Top
canapés with cucumber hearts and
sprinkle with salt and pepper. Serve
chilled or at room temperature.

THINK AHEAD
Assemble up to 3 hours in advance. Cover tightly
with plastic wrap and refrigerate.

SMOKED OYSTERS ON RYE CANAPES WITH SOUR CREAM AND TARRAGON

MAKES 20

20 drained smoked oysters

⅔ cup sour cream

1 recipe rye canapé bases (see page 52)

salt, black pepper

20 tarragon sprigs to garnish

Pat oysters dry with paper towels. Divide sour cream evenly among canapé bases. Place oyster on top and sprinkle with salt and pepper. Garnish with tarragon. Serve chilled or at room temperature.

THINK AHEAD
Top canapés up to 45 minutes in advance.

PARIS HAM WITH DIJON BUTTER CANAPES

MAKES 20

6 tbsp butter, softened

1 tsp Dijon mustard

1 recipe white bread canapé bases (see page 52)

7oz ham, thickly sliced

20 cornichon fans to garnish (see below)

ESSENTIAL EQUIPMENT
2-inch fluted pastry cutter

Mix butter and mustard. Spread on canapé bases. Cut out 20 rounds of ham with pastry cutter. Fold each ham round in half and place on canapés. Garnish with cornichon fans. Serve chilled or at room temperature.

THINK AHEAD
Top canapés up to 3 hours in advance. Cover tightly with plastic wrap and refrigerate.

CORNICHON FANS
Cut 10 cornichons in half lengthwise. Cut fine slices through each cornichon half, leaving slices attached at one end.

CARPACCIO CANAPES

MAKES 20

1 tbsp mayonnaise (see page 142)

dash of Worcestershire sauce

squeeze of lemon juice

1 tbsp milk

salt, white pepper

4oz beef fillet steak, 1-inch thick

1 recipe whole-wheat bread canapé bases (see page 52)

ESSENTIAL EQUIPMENT
paper piping cone (see page 146)

Combine mayonnaise, Worcestershire sauce, lemon, and milk. Add salt and pepper to taste. Cut steak across the grain into 2-inch-wide strips. Place strips end to end in a line on top of a piece of foil. Roll beef strips up tightly in the foil. Twist the ends of foil to give the beef strips a rounded shape. Chill for 20 minutes in freezer. Cut beef into ⅛-inch slices (see below, left). Flatten each slice by setting the blade of the knife on top and pressing down lightly. Divide beef slices among canapé bases. Fill paper piping cone with sauce and drizzle on canapes. Serve at room temperature.

THINK AHEAD
Make sauce up to 1 day in advance. Cover and refrigerate. Roll beef up to 1 day in advance; refrigerate. Top canapés up to 45 minutes in advance.

COOKS' NOTE
If you don't feel comfortable serving raw beef, rare roast beef slices can be used as an alternative. Use a 2-inch pastry cutter to cut the roast beef into rounds. Top canapés and drizzle with sauce.

BEET ROSTI WITH SMOKED TROUT AND HORSERADISH MOUSSE

MAKES 20

FOR MOUSSE
½ lb smoked trout
4oz cream cheese
1 tbsp horseradish sauce
1 tbsp lemon juice
cayenne pepper

ESSENTIAL EQUIPMENT
9-inch nonstick frying pan, 1 ¾ -inch fluted pastry cutter; piping bag with a large star nozzle

FOR ROSTI
1¼ cups grated cooked or canned beets
1¼ cups grated potato, peeled and squeezed dry
1 tbsp all-purpose flour
1 egg, beaten
¾ tsp salt, ¼ tsp black pepper
2 tbsp sunflower oil
paprika to garnish

For mousse, place trout, cream cheese, horseradish, and lemon juice in a food processor or blender; pulse to a smooth paste. Add cayenne pepper to taste. For rosti, mix beets, potato, flour, egg, salt, and pepper together. Heat 1 tbsp oil in the nonstick pan. Spread half the potato mixture, ¼-inch thick, across the bottom of the pan. Reduce heat to low and cook until both sides are crisp and golden, about 10 minutes per side. Remove from pan and cool slightly on paper towels. Heat the remaining oil. Cook and cool the remaining potato mixture. Cut out 10 rounds from each rosti with the pastry cutter (see opposite, middle). Cool completely before topping. Fill piping bag with mousse and pipe onto rostis (see page 146). Sprinkle with paprika to garnish. Serve at room temperature.

THINK AHEAD
Make mousse up to 3 days in advance. Cover and refrigerate. Make rosti rounds up to 2 days in advance. Store in layers on waxed paper in an airtight container in the refrigerator. Crisp in preheated 400°F oven for 5 minutes. Top and garnish up to 1 hour before serving.

Stamp out rounds from each rosti.

POTATO ROSTI WITH CREME FRAICHE, CAVIAR, AND DILL

MAKES 20

1lb potatoes, grated, peeled, and squeezed dry
1 tsp flour
¾ tsp salt, ¼ tsp black pepper
2 tbsp sunflower oil
½ cup crème fraîche or sour cream
⅓ cup black lumpfish caviar
20 dill sprigs to garnish

ESSENTIAL EQUIPMENT
9-inch nonstick frying pan, 1 ¾ -inch plain pastry cutter

Mix potato, flour, salt, and pepper together. Heat 1 tbsp oil in the nonstick pan. Spread half the potato mixture, ¼-inch thick, across the bottom of the pan. Reduce heat to low and cook until both sides are crisp and golden, about 10 minutes per side. Remove from pan and cool slightly on paper towels. Heat the remaining oil. Cook and cool the remaining potato mixture.
Cut out 10 rounds from each rosti with the pastry cutter (see opposite, middle). Cool completely before topping. Top mini rostis with 1 tsp each crème fraîche or sour cream and caviar. Garnish with dill sprigs. Serve warm.

THINK AHEAD
Make rosti rounds up to 2 days in advance. Store in layers on waxed paper in an airtight container in the refrigerator. Crisp in preheated 400°F oven for 5 minutes. Top up to 45 minutes before serving.

MINI LATKES WITH SOUR CREAM AND APPLE SAUCE

MAKES 20

1lb potatoes, peeled, grated,
  and squeezed dry
1 onion, grated and squeezed dry
1 tbsp all-purpose flour
1 egg, beaten
¾ tsp salt, ¼ tsp black pepper
2 tbsp sunflower oil
½ cup sour cream
½ cup apple sauce
2 tbsp finely chopped chives

Mix potatoes, onion, flour, egg, salt, and pepper together. Heat oil in a frying pan over medium heat. Working in batches, drop heaped teaspoonfuls of mixture into the hot oil. Use the back of spoon to flatten them into thin pancakes. Cook, turning once, until crisp and golden on each side. Drain on paper towels. Cool slightly before topping. Top latkes with 1 tsp each sour cream and apple sauce. Garnish with chopped chives. Serve warm or at room temperature.

THINK AHEAD
Make latkes up to 2 days in advance. Store in layers on waxed paper in an airtight container in the refrigerator. Crisp in preheated 400°F oven for 5 minutes. Top up to 45 minutes before serving.

COOKS' NOTE
The oaky, salty flavor of smoked fish perfectly complements these crispy potato pancakes. Try the classic combination of smoked salmon, sour cream, and a squeeze of lemon.

CRISPY CARROT AND SCALLION CAKES WITH FETA AND BLACK OLIVE

MAKES 20

2 cups grated carrots
1¼ cups peeled grated potatoes,
  squeezed dry
2 scallions, finely chopped
1 tbsp all-purpose flour
1 egg, beaten
¾ tsp salt, ¼ tsp black pepper
2 tbsp sunflower oil
¾ cup feta cheese, crumbled
10 pitted black olives, quartered

Mix carrot, potato, scallion, flour, egg, and salt and pepper together. Heat oil in a frying pan over medium heat. Working in batches, drop heaping teaspoonfuls of mixture into the hot oil. Use the back of the spoon to flatten them into thin pancakes. Cook, turning once, until crisp and golden on each side, 5 minutes per side. Drain on paper towels. Cool to room temperature before topping. Divide feta cheese and olives among the cakes. Serve at room temperature.

THINK AHEAD
Make up to 2 days in advance. Store in layers on paper towels in an airtight container at room temperature. Crisp in 400°F oven for 3 minutes. Top 45 minutes before serving.

BABY BAKED POTATOES WITH SOUR CREAM AND CAVIAR

MAKES 20

20 tiny new potatoes, pricked
1 tbsp olive oil
2 tsp salt
½ cup sour cream
⅓ cup black lumpfish caviar

Preheat oven to 400°F.
Toss potatoes with oil and salt until evenly coated. Place on a baking sheet and cook until soft inside and crisp outside, about 30 minutes. Cool completely. Cut a cross on top of each potato and squeeze gently to open. Top each baby potato with 1 tsp each sour cream and caviar. Serve immediately.

THINK AHEAD
Bake potatoes up to 1 day in advance. Store in an airtight container in the refrigerator. Crisp in a preheated 400°F oven for 5 minutes. Top just before serving.

KIWI AND PASSION-FRUIT MINI PAVLOVAS

MAKES 20

1 recipe baked vanilla mini meringues
(see page 141)
⅓ cup heavy cream
1 tbsp granualted sugar
1 kiwi, peeled
2 passion fruit, halved
20 raspberries
2 tsp powdered sugar for dusting

Whip cream until it holds soft peaks. Whisk in 1 tbsp granulated sugar (see page 144). Cut kiwi in half and cut each half into 5 slices. Cut each slice in half. Scoop out pulp from passion fruit halves. Top each pavlova with 1 tsp cream. Arrange a half kiwi slice and a raspberry on top. Topo with passion fruit pulp and dust with powdered sugar.

THINK AHEAD
Assemble meringues up to 3 hours in advance; store at room temperature.

MUSCOVADO AND FIG MINI MERINGUES

MAKES 20

1 recipe baked muscovado mini meringues
(see page 141)
2 figs
2oz plain chocolate, melted
(see page 145)
½ cup crème fraîche or sour cream
2 tsp cocoa powder for dusting

Cut figs in half, then slice each half into 5 slivers. Top individual meringues with 1 tsp crème fraîche and dust lightly with cocoa powder. Arrange 1 fig sliver on top then, using a teaspoon, drizzle with melted chocolate. Serve at room temperature.

THINK AHEAD
Assemble meringues up to 3 hours in advance; store at room temperature.

STRAWBERRY AND PISTACHIO MINI MERINGUES

MAKES 20

1 recipe baked pistachio mini meringues
(see page 141)
5 strawberries
⅓ cup heavy cream
1 tbsp granulated sugar
2 tsp powdered sugar for dusting
2 tbsp chopped pistachios to garnish

Cut strawberries into quarters. Whip cream until it holds soft peaks. Whisk in 1 tbsp granulated sugar (see page 144). Top each meringue with 1 tsp cream and dust with powdered sugar. Arrange strawberry quarters on top. Garnish with chopped pistachios.

THINK AHEAD
Assemble meringues 3 hours before serving; store at room temperature.

HAZELNUT AND RASPBERRY MINI MERINGUES

MAKES 20

1 recipe baked hazlenut mini meringues
(see page 141)
⅓ cup heavy cream
1 tbsp granulated sugar
2 cups raspberries
2 tsp powdered sugar for dusting
20 tiny mint sprigs to garnish

Whip cream until it holds soft peaks. Whisk in sugar (see page 144). Top each pavlova with 1 tsp cream. Arrange raspberries on top and dust with powdered sugar. Garnish with mint sprigs.

THINK AHEAD
Assemble meringues up to 3 hours in advance; keep at room temperature.

POLENTA CROSTINI

MAKES 20

3 ⅔ cups water
1 ¼ cups instant polenta
1 tsp salt
4 tbsp grated Parmesan cheese
½ tsp black pepper
2 tbsp olive oil

ESSENTIAL EQUIPMENT
1lb oiled loaf tin

Bring water to a boil in a large pan. Stir in the polenta and salt. Cook, stirring constantly, until thick, 5–10 minutes. Add Parmesan and pepper. Pour hot polenta into the greased loaf pan (see below). After cooling completely, unmold from the pan. Slice into 10 slices (see below). Cut each slice diagonally into 2 triangles. Place triangles onto oiled baking sheets. Brush with oil. Toast under a preheated broiler until lightly golden and crisp, 3 minutes. Cool to room temperature before topping.

THINK AHEAD
Make polenta up to 3 days in advance, leaving it in the pan. Cover and refrigerate. Cut and broil polenta up to 2 hours in advance. Store at room temperature.

COOKS' NOTE
Add 2 crushed garlic cloves and 1 tbsp finely chopped herbs—rosemary, thyme, or oregano—to the cooked, hot polenta for a little extra flavor.

Pour into an oiled loaf pan.

Unmold polenta from the tin and slice.

POLENTA CROSTINI WITH BLUE CHEESE AND BALSAMIC RED ONIONS

MAKES 20

2 tbsp olive oil
2 medium red onions, thinly sliced
½ tsp salt
1 tbsp balsamic vinegar
black pepper
1 recipe polenta crostini (see left)
1 cup crumbled Danish blue cheese

Heat oil in a pan over medium heat. Add onions and salt. Cook, stirring occasionally, until soft and tender, 10 minutes. Add vinegar and cook until evaporated, 3 minutes. Add pepper to taste. Cool to room temperature. Divide onions evenly among crostini, then top each one with 1 tsp crumbled cheese. Serve at room temperature.

THINK AHEAD
Cook onions up to 1 day in advance. Cover and store at room temperature. Top crostini 1 hour in advance. Store at room temperature.

POLENTA CROSTINI WITH TOMATO AND BLACK OLIVE SALSA

MAKES 20

2 ripe tomatoes, peeled, seeded, and diced (see page 147)
1 medium red onion, finely chopped
¼ cup finely chopped pitted black olives
2 tsp olive oil
1 tsp red wine vinegar
salt, pepper
1 recipe polenta crostini (see far left)

Combine tomatoes, onion, olives, oil, and vinegar. Add salt and pepper to taste. Cover and let stand at room temperature for 30 minutes to allow the flavors to blend.
Top polenta crostini with salsa. Serve at room temperature.

THINK AHEAD
Make salsa up to 1 day in advance but do not add salt and pepper until just before using. Store in an airtight container in the refrigerator. Top crostini 1 hour in advance. Store at room temperature.

TOSTADITAS

MAKES 24

3 - 6-inch flour tortillas
½ tbsp sunflower oil
¼ tsp salt

Preheat oven to 400°F.
Brush tortillas on one side with oil.
Cut each tortilla into 8 even-sized
wedges with kitchen scissors or a
serrated knife. Arrange oiled side up
in a single layer on an oiled baking
sheet. Sprinkle with salt. Bake
until crisp, 5–7 minutes. Cool on a
wire rack.

THINK AHEAD
Make tostaditas up to 5 days in advance. Store
in an airtight container at room temperature.

COOKS' NOTE
Good-quality store-bought corn chips can be
used as a time-saving alternative. Be sure to
buy plain, lightly salted chips, not ones that are
flavored with spices. A flavored chip won't allow
you to appreciate the delicious topping.

TOSTADITAS WITH ROAST CORN SALSA

MAKES 24
½ corn on the cob
½ red pepper, seeded and quartered
½ green chili, seeded and finely chopped
½ medium red onion, finely chopped
1 tbsp finely chopped cilantro leaves
1 tbsp lime juice
1 tbsp olive oil
salt, black pepper
1 recipe tostaditas (see opposite)

Preheat oven to 350°F.
Rinse corn under cold water to moisten. Place corn and pepper quarters on a sheet
pan. Roast for 25 minutes. Remove pepper and peel and seed (see page 147). Roast
corn for another 20 minutes.
Finely dice the pepper. When corn is cool, cut the roasted kernels from the cob with
a sharp knife. Combine corn, peppers, chili, onion, cilantro, lime, and oil. Add salt
and pepper to taste. Cover and refrigerate for 1 hour to allow flavors to blend. Top
tostaditas with salsa. Serve chilled or at room temperature.

THINK AHEAD
Make salsa up to 1 day in advance, but do not add the cilantro more than 3 hours before serving. Cover and
refrigerate. Top tostaditas and serve immediately.

COOKS' NOTE
Oven roasting the corn is an important step since it allows the natural sugar in the corn to caramelize. It also
adds a nutty, smoky flavor to the corn's natural sweetness.

MINI POPPADOMS WITH CREAMY CHICKEN TIKKA

MAKES 30

30 mini poppadoms (see Cooks' Note)
1 tbsp sunflower oil
1 boneless, skinless chicken breast
1-inch piece fresh ginger, grated
1 garlic clove, crushed
½ tsp ground cardamon
½ tsp ground cumin
½ tsp salt, ¼ tsp black pepper
1 tbsp lemon juice
4 tbsp whole-milk yogurt
½ tsp paprika for sprinkling
30 cilantro leaves to garnish

Preheat oven to 400°F.
Place mini poppadoms in a single layer
on an greased baking sheet. Brush
with oil. Bake until crisp and golden,
3–5 minutes. Cool on a wire rack.
Cut chicken into ¼-inch thick slices.
Combine chicken, ginger, garlic, spices,
salt, pepper, lemon juice, and yogurt in a
nonmetallic bowl. Cover and refrigerate
for at least 1 hour.
Place chicken under a preheated grill
until cooked through, 8–10 minutes.
Cool. Roughly chop.
Divide chicken evenly among the
poppadoms. Sprinkle with paprika and
garnish with cilantro leaves. Serve
chilled or at room temperature.

THINK AHEAD
Bake poppadoms up to 2 days in advance. Store in
an airtight container at room temperature. Marinate
chicken up to 1 day in advance. Cook chicken up to
1 day in advance. Cover and refrigerate. Top
poppadoms up to 1 hour before serving.

COOKS' NOTE
Poppadoms are wafer-thin Indian flatbreads.
They come in many flavors and sizes. Look for mini
poppadoms at gourmet food stores and Indian
markets. If you have difficulty finding them, this
Indian-inspired topping is also delicious served
on tostaditas.

TOSTADITAS WITH CITRUS CEVICHE

MAKES 24

¼ lb halibut fillet
juice of 1 lime
juice of ½ lemon
2 tbsp orange juice
1 red chili, seeded and finely chopped
1 scallion, white stem only, finely chopped
1 tomato, seeded and diced (see page 147)
1 small avocado, peeled, pitted, and diced
2 tbsp finely chopped cilantro leaves
½ tsp salt
1 recipe tostaditas (see page 59)
cilantro leaves to garnish

Cut the fish into fine dice. Combine
fish with the lime, lemon, and orange
juices in a nonmetallic bowl. Cover
and refrigerate for 3 hours, stirring
occasionally. Drain fish well, discarding
all but 1 tbsp marinade. Toss the fish,
chili, scallion, tomato, avocado, cilantro,
salt, and reserved 1 tbsp marinade
together to combine. Top tostaditas
with equal amounts of the ceviche.
Garnish with cilantro leaves.
Serve chilled.

THINK AHEAD
Make ceviche up to 1 day in advance, but do
not add the avocado, salt, and cilantro more than
3 hours before serving. Press plastic wrap tightly
over the surface of the ceviche and refrigerate. Top
tostaditas just before serving.

COOKS' NOTE
Fresh tuna, salmon, or scallops also make excellent
ceviche. Use cooked shrimp if you prefer not to use
raw fish.

TOSTADITAS WITH BLACKENED SNAPPER, PEACH RELISH, AND SOUR CREAM

MAKES 24

¼ tsp dried thyme
¼ tsp dried oregano
¼ tsp paprika
¼ tsp cumin seeds
¼ tsp garlic powder
½ tsp salt, ¼ tsp black pepper
¼ lb red snapper fillet, ½-inch thick
2 tsp sunflower oil
1 pitted peach, fresh or canned, finely diced
2 tsp lemon juice
1 recipe tostaditas (see page 59)
5 tbsp sour cream to garnish

Combine thyme, oregano, paprika,
cumin, garlic, salt and pepper on a plate.
Cut fish into 24 - ½-inch cubes. Dip fish
first in oil, then roll in spice mixture.
Preheat a dry frying pan over a medium
heat until very hot. Add fish cubes,
spiced side down. Cook cubes 2 minutes
per side until firm to the touch. Remove
from pan and cool.
For relish, combine peach and lemon
juice. Divide relish evenly among
tostaditas. Top with fish. Garnish with
sour cream. Serve chilled or at
room temperature.

THINK AHEAD
Cook fish up to 1 day in advance. Cover and
refrigerate. Make relish up to 1 day in advance.
Cover and refrigerate. Top tostaditas up to 45
minutes before serving.

GINGERED CHICKEN CAKES WITH CILANTRO-LIME MAYONNAISE

MAKES 20

FOR CAKES

2 boneless, skinless chicken breasts

2 tbsp fish sauce

1-inch piece fresh ginger, roughly chopped

3 scallions, roughly chopped

1 garlic clove, crushed

1 tsp salt, ¼ tsp tabasco

FOR TOPPING

4 tbsp mayonnaise (see page 142)

¼ cup finely chopped cilantro leaves

juice of 1 lime

2 tbsp diced mango (see page 163) to garnish

20 cilantro leaves to garnish

Preheat oven to 400°F.

For cakes, place all cake ingredients in a food processor or blender; pulse until finely minced. Divide mixture into 20 walnut-sized pieces. With wet hands, shape each piece into a ball and flatten into a cake. Place cakes on an oiled baking sheet and bake until golden and cooked through, 12 minutes. Cool to warm or room temperature.

For topping, combine mayonnaise, cilantro, and lime. Spoon topping on to cakes. Garnish with diced mango and cilantro leaves. Serve warm or at room temperature.

THINK AHEAD

Assemble cakes and prepare topping up to 1 day in advance. Cover and refrigerate. Bake and top cakes up to 1 hour in advance. Keep at room temperature. Garnish and serve.

COOKS' NOTE

Try using pork fillet instead of chicken and lemon grass instead of ginger for a tasty variation on these Asian-inspired minced cakes.

COCKTAIL SALMON AND DILL CAKES WITH CREME FRAICHE TARTARE

MAKES 20

FOR CAKES

⅓ lb salmon fillet

½ lb potato, peeled

2 tbsp roughly chopped dill

2 tbsp tomato ketchup

1 tsp horseradish sauce

1 tsp lemon juice

1 tsp salt, ¼ tsp tabasco

2 tbsp fresh breadcrumbs

FOR TOPPING

4 tbsp crème fraîche or sour cream

1 tsp drained capers, finely chopped

1 tsp drained cocktail gherkins, finely chopped

1 tsp finely chopped tarragon

salt, black pepper

20 watercress, tarragon, or parsley sprigs to garnish

Place salmon in pan of boiling water. Return water to a boil, then remove pan from heat at once. Cool thoroughly. Drain on paper towels. Separate cooked salmon into large flakes.

Preheat oven to 400°F. Cook potato in boiling water until tender. Remove and mash until smooth. Combine potatoes with salmon, dill, ketchup, horseradish sauce, and lemon. Add salt and pepper to taste. Divide mixture into 20 walnut-sized pieces. Shape pieces into balls and roll in breadcrumbs. Flatten into cakes and place on an oiled baking sheet. Bake until golden, 10 minutes. Cool to warm or room temperature. For topping, combine all topping ingredients. Add salt and tabasco and mix well. Spoon topping onto cakes. Garnish with watercress. Serve warm or at room temperature.

THINK AHEAD

Assemble cakes and prepare topping up to 1 day in advance. Cover and refrigerate. Bake and top cakes up to 1 hour in advance. Store at room temperature. Garnish just before serving.

MINI DEVILED CRAB CAKES WITH TOMATO REMOULADE

MAKES 20

FOR CAKES
½ lb crab meat
½ onion, finely chopped
½ tsp honey
½ tsp mustard powder
½ tsp tabasco
1 tsp horseradish sauce
1 tsp Worcestershire sauce
1 tsp lemon juice
3 tbsp mayonnaise (see page 142)
7–9 tbsp fresh breadcrumbs
salt, black pepper

FOR TOPPING
4 tbsp mayonnaise (see page 142)
2 tsp finely chopped chives
1 tsp lemon juice
½ tsp Dijon mustard
½ tsp garlic, finely chopped
salt, black pepper
1 tomato, peeled, seeded, chopped, and diced (see page 147)
finely chopped chives to garnish

For cakes, mix crab, onion, honey, mustard powder, Worcestershire and horseradish sauces, lemon juice, and mayonnaise together. Add enough fresh breadcrumbs to bind, about 2–4 tbsp. Add salt and pepper to taste. Divide mixture into heaping teaspoonfuls, about 20 walnut-sized pieces. Shape each piece into a ball and roll lightly in remaining crumbs. Place on an oiled baking sheet. Refrigerate until firm, 30 minutes. Preheat oven to 400°F. Bake crab cakes until crisp and golden, 10 minutes. Cool to warm or room temperature.

For topping, combine mayonnaise, chives, lemon juice, mustard, and garlic. Add salt and pepper to taste. Spoon topping onto crab cakes. Garnish with tomato and chives. Serve warm or at room temperature.

THINK AHEAD
Assemble cakes and make topping up to 1 day in advance. Cover and refrigerate
Bake and top cakes up to 1 hour before serving.

EGGPLANT AND PINE NUT FRITTERS WITH ROASTED TOMATO SAUCE

MAKES 20

FOR TOPPING
2 plum tomatoes, halved
1 garlic clove, sliced
1 tsp balsamic vinegar
½ tsp honey
½ tsp finely chopped rosemary leaves
salt, black pepper

FOR FRITTERS
2 tbsp olive oil
1 medium eggplant, diced
1 garlic clove, crushed
1 tbsp finely chopped parsley leaves
1 tsp finely chopped rosemary leaves
1 egg plus 1 egg yolk, beaten
1 cup grated Parmesan cheese
1 cup diced mozzarella cheese
½ cup dry breadcrumbs
½ cup pine nuts, roughly chopped
salt, black pepper
20 small arugula leaves to garnish

Preheat oven to 400°F.
For topping, put tomatoes and garlic in a baking pan. Drizzle with vinegar and honey and sprinkle with rosemary, salt, and pepper. Roast in oven until softened, 20 minutes. Cool and place in a food processor or blender; pulse until smooth, reserve. For fritters, heat oil in a skillet over medium-high heat. Stir-fry diced eggplant until soft and golden, 10 minutes. Drain and cool on paper towels. Combine with garlic, parsley, rosemary, beaten eggs, Parmesan, mozzarella, breadcrumbs, and pine nuts. Add salt and pepper to taste. Divide mixture into 20 walnut-sized pieces. Shape each piece into an oval. Place ovals on an oiled baking sheet. Bake until golden, 10 minutes. Cool to warm or room temperature. Spoon topping onto cakes. Garnish with arugula. Serve warm or at room temperature.

THINK AHEAD
Assemble fritters and prepare topping up to 1 day in advance. Cover and refrigerate. Cook and top fritters up to 1 hour in advance. Store at room temperature. Garnish just before serving.

MINI STICKY ORANGE AND ALMOND CAKES

MAKES 25

2 whole oranges, unpeeled

6 eggs, beaten

1¼ cups granulated sugar

1¾ cups ground almonds

1 tsp baking powder

⅔ cup whole-milk yogurt

4 tbsp pomegranate seeds (see below)
  to garnish

powdered sugar, to garnish

ESSENTIAL EQUIPMENT

14 x 10-inch jelly-roll pan lined with buttered baking parchment, 1½-inch pastry cutter

Cook whole oranges in boiling water until soft, 1½ hours. Cool completely. Preheat oven to 375°F.

For cake, cut oranges in half and remove any seeds. Place in a food processor; process to a smooth purée. Add eggs, sugar, almonds and baking powder; pulse until well blended. Pour batter into the lined pan. Bake until firm to the touch, 40 minutes. Cool completely. Cut pomegranate in half through the middle of the stem end. Cut each half into quarters (see below, top right). Pull stem ends of each quarter towards each other, bending peel back to release pomegranate seeds (see below, bottom right). Cut cake into 20 rounds with the pastry cutter (see below, left). Spoon ½ tsp yogurt onto each cake round. Garnish with pomegranate seeds and sprinkle with powdered sugar. Serve at room temperature.

THINK AHEAD

Make cake up to 2 days in advance. Store at room temperature. Alternatively, freeze cake up to 1 month in advance (see page 149). Defrost in the refrigerator overnight. Glaze cakes up to 3 hours ahead. Leave at room temperature, until ready to serve.

Stamp out cake rounds.

Cut pomegranate into quarters.

Pull back peel to release kernels.

MINI CHOCOLATE TRUFFLE CAKES

MAKES 25

FOR CAKE

14oz dark chocolate, broken into pieces

10 tbsp butter

¾ cup granulated sugar

5 eggs, separated

⅓ cup all-purpose flour

FOR GLAZE

5 tbsp heavy cream

2½ oz dark chocolate, broken into pieces

ESSENTIAL EQUIPMENT

14 x 10-inch jelly-roll pan lined with buttered baking parchment, 1¾-inch pastry cutter

Preheat oven to 300°F.

For cake, melt butter and chocolate together in a double boiler over low heat. Stir continuously until smooth and melted. Remove from heat and cool to lukewarm. Beat sugar, egg yolks, and flour into the cool chocolate. Whisk egg whites until they hold soft peaks (see page 141). Gently fold chocolate mixture into whites until evenly combined. Pour batter into the lined pan. Bake until firm to the touch, 20 minutes. Cool thoroughly.

For glaze, heat cream in a pan just below the boiling point. Remove from heat. Stir in chocolate until melted and smooth. Cool until slightly thickened, 30 minutes. Cut cooled cake into 25 rounds with the pastry cutter. Spoon 1 heaping teaspoonful of glaze over each cake round. Serve at room temperature.

THINK AHEAD

Bake cake up to 5 days in advance. Store at room temperature. Alternatively, bake and freeze cake up to 1 month in advance (see page 149). Defrost in refrigerator overnight. Cut and glaze cake rounds up to 3 hours in advance. Leave at room temperature, until ready to serve.

STICKS AND SKEWERS

PROSCIUTTO-WRAPPED SCALLOP BROCHETTES WITH SAUCE BEARNAISE

MAKES 20

20 bay scallops or 10 sea scallops
7 very thin prosciutto slices
20 large basil leaves
salt, black pepper
1 recipe sauce bearnaise (see page 143)

ESSENTIAL EQUIPMENT
20 - 6-inch wooden skewers presoaked in cold water

If using sea scallops, slice in half. Cut each prosciutto slice into 3 strips. Place 1 basil leaf on top of each prosciutto strip. Place 1 bay scallop or ½ sea scallop on top. Sprinkle with a pinch of both salt and pepper. Wrap basil and prosciutto around each scallop. Secure each wrapped scallop with 1 presoaked skewer.
Preheat broiler. Alternatively, preheat a ridged cast-iron griddle, or a barbecue grill. Broil, grill, or pan-griddle scallop brochettes until scallops have turned from opaque to white, 1–2 minutes on each side. Serve hot, warm or at room temperature with sauce bearnaise.

THINK AHEAD
Skewer scallops up to 8 hours in advance. Store in an airtight container in the refrigerator.

TANGY THAI SHRIMP SKEWERS

MAKES 20

20 tiger shrimp, cooked and peeled
2 garlic cloves, finely chopped
½-inch piece fresh ginger, grated
1 red chili, seeded and finely chopped
1 tsp granulated sugar
1 tbsp fish sauce
juice of 1 lime

ESSENTIAL EQUIPMENT
20 - 5-inch wooden skewers or toothpicks

Pat shrimp dry with paper towels. Combine shrimp, garlic, ginger, chili, sugar, sauce, and lime in a nonmetallic bowl. Cover and refrigerate for 1 hour. Skewer 1 shrimp on to each skewer. Serve chilled.

THINK AHEAD
Marinate shrimp up to 6 hours in advance. Skewer shrimp up to 3 hours in advance. Store in an airtight container in the refrigerator.

COOKS' NOTE ON GRILLING WITH SKEWERS

Don't forget to presoak wooden skewers when using them in a recipe calling for broiling or grilling. Allow the skewers to soak for at least 30 minutes in cold water to prevent them from scorching.

BARBECUED TANDOORI PRAWN STICKS

MAKES 20

½ cup whole-milk yogurt
2 tbsp lemon juice
3 garlic cloves, crushed
1-inch piece fresh ginger, grated
1 tsp turmeric
1 tsp paprika
¼ tsp ground cardamom
¼ tsp cayenne pepper, 1 tsp salt
20 raw tiger shrimp, peeled and deveined (see page 164)

ESSENTIAL EQUIPMENT
20 - 3-inch wooden skewers or toothpicks presoaked in cold water

For marinade, combine yogurt, lemon juice, garlic, ginger, spices, and salt in a nonmetallic bowl. Add shrimp and toss in marinade to coat each one well. Cover and refrigerate for 1 hour. Thread 1 shrimp onto each presoaked skewer. Preheat broiler. Alternatively, preheat a ridged cast-iron griddle, grill pan or barbecue. Grill or broil shrimp until they turn pink and lose their transparency, 3 minutes on each side. Serve hot, warm or at room temperature.

THINK AHEAD
Marinate shrimp up to 4 hours in advance. Store in an airtight container in the refrigerator. Skewer shrimp up to 1 hour in advance. Store in an airtight container in the refrigerator.

GRAPEFRUIT SCALLOP CEVICHE SKEWERS

MAKES 20

40 bay scallops or 20 sea scallops
grated zest and juice of 1 grapefruit
juice of 2 limes
4 tbsp olive oil
1 fresh red chili, seeded and finely
  chopped
½ red onion, finely chopped
½ tsp salt
1 tbsp finely chopped cilantro leaves
1 scallion, finely sliced

ESSENTIAL EQUIPMENT
20 - 5-inch wooden skewers or toothpicks

If using sea scallops, slice in half
crosswise. Combine scallops, grapefruit
juice and zest, lime, oil, chili, onion, and
salt in a nonmetallic bowl. Cover and
refrigerate for 3 hours, stirring
occasionally. Remove scallops with a
slotted spoon. Toss to coat with cilantro
and scallion. Thread 2 bay scallops or
2 sea scallop halves onto each skewer.
Serve chilled.

THINK AHEAD
Marinate scallops up to 6 hours in advance. Skewer
scallops up to 3 hours in advance. Store in an
airtight container in the refrigerator.

COOKS' NOTE
If you are uncomfortable about serving raw fish, use
cooked, peeled tiger shrimp instead of raw scallops.

LEMON CHILI SHRIMP STICKS

MAKES 20

2 garlic cloves, crushed
½-inch piece fresh ginger, grated
2 tbsp finely chopped cilantro leaves
½ tbsp Chinese hot chili sauce
1 tbsp light soy sauce
1 tbsp honey
3 tbsp lemon juice
20 raw medium shrimp, peeled and deveined (see page 164)

ESSENTIAL EQUIPMENT
20 - 6-inch wooden skewers presoaked in cold water

For marinade, combine garlic, ginger, cilantro, chili sauce, soy sauce, honey, and
lemon juice in a nonmetallic bowl. Add shrimp and toss in marinade to coat each
one well. Cover and refrigerate for 1 hour. Thread 1 shrimp onto each presoaked
skewer. Preheat broiler. Alternatively, preheat a ridged cast-iron griddle, broiler pan,
or barbecue. Broil or grill shrimp until they turn pink and lose their transparency,
3 minutes on each side. Serve hot, warm or at room temperature.

THINK AHEAD
Marinate shrimp up to 4 hours in advance. Store in an airtight container in the refrigerator. Skewer shrimp up
to 1 hour in advance. Store in an airtight container in the refrigerator.

SHRIMP AND SUGARCANE STICKS WITH MINTED CHILI DIPPING SAUCE

MAKES 20

4 - 4-inch-long sugarcane pieces	1 tsp salt
1lb raw shrimp, peeled and deveined (see page 164)	½ tsp black pepper
2 garlic cloves, chopped	**FOR SAUCE**
3 scallions, chopped	1 tbsp finely chopped mint
1 tbsp fish sauce	1 fresh green chili, seeded and finely chopped
1 tsp sugar	1 tbsp sugar
1 tbsp cornstarch	6 tbsp lime juice
1 egg white	6 tbsp fish sauce

Peel sugarcane with a vegetable peeler. Cut each sugarcane piece into ¼-inch-thick strips to make 20 sugarcane sticks (see page 148). Place shrimp, garlic, scallion, fish sauce, sugar, cornstarch, egg white, salt, and pepper in a food processor or blender; pulse to a smooth paste. Divide shrimp paste into 20 equal-sized pieces. With wet hands, place 1 piece of shrimp paste in the middle of your palm. Place sugarcane stick in the middle of the paste. Mold shrimp paste around the end of the stick. Repeat with remaining paste and sticks. Cover shrimp sticks and refrigerate for 30 minutes.

For sauce, combine mint, chili, sugar, lime, and fish sauce. Let stand at room temperature for 15 minutes to allow the flavors to blend.

Preheat broiler or barbecue. Broil shrimp sticks until golden and cooked through, 3 minutes on each side. Serve warm.

THINK AHEAD
Mold shrimp paste on to sugarcane sticks up to 4 hours in advance. Store in an airtight container in the refrigerator. Make dipping sauce without mint up to 3 days in advance. Cover and refrigerate. Add mint up to 3 hours before serving. Keep covered at room temperature.

COOKS' NOTE
You can find fresh, frozen, or canned sugarcane from Asian food stores. Wooden skewers are less exotic, but can be used for this fragrant shrimp paste.

SNOW PEA-WRAPPED SHRIMP SKEWERS WITH LEMON MAYONNAISE

MAKES 20
20 large snow peas
20 large shrimp, cooked and peeled
1 recipe lemon mayonnaise (see page 142)

ESSENTIAL EQUIPMENT
20 - 6-inch wooden skewers

Bring a pan of water to a boil over high heat. Add snow peas and boil for 1 minute. Drain and refresh them in cold water. Drain again and pat dry with paper towels.

Place 1 shrimp on top of each snow pea. Thread onto skewer. Cover and refrigerate for 30 minutes. Serve chilled with lemon mayonnaise.

THINK AHEAD
Skewer shrimp and snow peas up to 8 hours in advance. Store in an airtight container in the refrigerator.

SALMON TERIYAKI SKEWERS WITH GINGER SOY DIPPING SAUCE

MAKES 20

¾ lb salmon fillet, 1-inch thick

FOR GLAZE

3 tbsp sake

3 tbsp mirin

5 tbsp shoyu (Japanese soy sauce)

1½ tbsp sugar

FOR SAUCE

½-inch piece fresh ginger finely chopped

2 scallions, finely sliced

juice of 2 limes

6 tbsp shoyu

ESSENTIAL EQUIPMENT

20 - 6-inch wooden skewers or chopsticks presoaked in cold water

Cut salmon into 1-inch cubes.

For glaze, place sake, mirin, soy, and sugar in a small pan. Bring to a boil over medium heat. Simmer gently for 10 minutes until thick and syrupy. Cool.

For sauce, mix ginger, scallions, lime juice, and soy together. Let stand at room temperature for 15 minutes to allow the flavors to blend.

Toss salmon with cooled glaze in a nonmetallic bowl to coat each piece well. Let marinate at room temperature for 10 minutes. Thread 1 salmon cube onto 2 skewers or chopsticks.

Preheat broiler. Alternatively, preheat a ridged cast-iron griddle, broil pan, or barbecue. Grill or broil salmon skewers until firm to the touch, 2–3 minutes on each side. Serve hot or warm with ginger soy dipping sauce.

THINK AHEAD

Skewer salmon up to 3 hours in advance. Store in an airtight container in the refrigerator. Make dipping sauce without scallions up to 3 days in advance. Cover and refrigerate. Add scallions up to 3 hours before serving. Keep covered at room temperature.

COOK'S NOTE

Don't forget to presoak wooden skewers when using them in a grilled recipe. Allowing the skewers to soak for at least 30 minutes in cold water will prevent them from scorching.

MONKFISH, PANCETTA, AND ROSEMARY SPIEDINI WITH LEMON AIOLI

MAKES 20

¾ lb monkfish tail, boned, and skinned

4 pancetta or bacon slices

20 - 4-inch rosemary branches

FOR MARINADE

4 tbsp olive oil

grated zest and juice of ½ lemon

1 garlic clove, sliced

1 tsp salt, ½ tsp black pepper

1 recipe lemon aioli (see page 142)

Cut the monkfish into 20 - 1-inch cubes. Cut pancetta into 20 equal-sized pieces. Cover pancetta or bacon and refrigerate.

For rosemary skewers, pull the leaves off the rosemary stalks, leaving just a few leaves at one end. Reserve leaves. Sharpen the other end into a point with a sharp paring knife (see page 148). For marinade, roughly chop the reserved rosemary leaves. Combine rosemary, oil, lemon, garlic, salt, and pepper in a nonmetallic bowl. Add monkfish and toss to coat each piece well. Cover and refrigerate for 30 minutes.

Thread 1 monkfish cube and 1 bacon piece onto the pointed end of each rosemary skewer. Preheat broiler. Alternatively, preheat a ridged cast-iron griddle, broiler pan, or barbecue. Broil or grill monkfish spiedini until cooked through, 2–3 minutes on each side. Serve warm with lemon aioli.

THINK AHEAD

Marinate monkfish up to 4 hours in advance. Store in an airtight container in the refrigerator. Skewer up to 2 hours in advance. Store in an airtight container in the refrigerator.

COOKS' NOTE

If you are using an overhead grill to cook the spiedini, make sure that the rosemary-sprigged end protrudes from the oven so they do not catch fire.

MOROCCAN SPICED SWORDFISH BROCHETTES

MAKES 20

¾ lb swordfish steak, 1 inch thick

FOR MARINADE

1 red pepper, quartered and seeded
1 red chili, seeded and chopped
2 garlic cloves, chopped
2 tbsp chopped cilantro
2 tbsp chopped parsley
½ tsp ground coriander
1 tsp honey
grated zest and juice of ½ lemon
2 tbsp olive oil
1 tsp salt, ¼ tsp black pepper

ESSENTIAL EQUIPMENT
20 - 6-inch wooden skewers presoaked in cold water

Cut swordfish into 20 - 1-inch cubes. For marinade, broil and peel pepper quarters (see page 147). Place peeled pepper quarters, chili, garlic, fresh herbs, ground coriander, honey, lemon juice and zest, oil and salt and pepper in a food processor or blender; pulse to a thick paste. Toss swordfish and marinade together in a nonmetallic bowl to coat each piece well. Cover and refrigerate for at least 30 minutes. Thread 1 swordfish cube on to each presoaked skewer.
Preheat broiler. Alternatively, preheat a ridged cast-iron griddle, broiler pan or barbecue. Broil or grill swordfish brochettes until cooked through, 2–3 minutes on each side. Serve hot or warm.

THINK AHEAD
Marinate swordfish up to 4 hours in advance. Store in an airtight container in the refrigerator. Skewer up to 2 hours in advance. Store in an airtight container in the refrigerator.

CHARBROILED MEDITERRANEAN TUNA SKEWERS WITH SPICY ROAST TOMATO DIP

MAKES 20

¾ lb tuna steak, 1-inch thick

FOR MARINADE

1 cup basil leaves
1 cup parsley leaves
2 garlic cloves
grated zest and juice of ½ lemon
2 tbsp olive oil
1 tsp salt
½ tsp black pepper
20 large basil leaves

FOR DIP

6 plum tomatoes, halved
1 red chili, seeded and chopped
2 garlic cloves, chopped
1 tbsp olive oil
1 tbsp balsamic vinegar
salt, black pepper

ESSENTIAL EQUIPMENT
20 - 6-inch wooden skewers presoaked in cold water

For marinade, place basil, parsley, garlic, lemon zest and juice, oil, salt, and pepper in a food processor or blender; pulse to a thick paste. Toss tuna and marinade together in a nonmetallic bowl to coat each piece well. Cover and refrigerate for at least 30 minutes.
For dip, preheat oven to 400°F. Place tomatoes on an sheet pan. Sprinkle with chili, garlic, oil, vinegar, and a pinch each salt and pepper. Roast until softened, 30 minutes. Place in a food processor or blender; pulse until smooth. Push through a strainer to remove seeds. Add salt and pepper to taste. Keep warm.
Cut tuna into 1-inch cubes. Wrap each tuna cube in a basil leaf. Thread 1 wrapped tuna cube onto each presoaked skewer. Preheat broiler.
Alternatively, preheat a ridged cast-iron griddle, broiler pan or barbecue. Broil or grill tuna skewers until cooked through, 2–3 minutes on each side. Serve hot or warm with spicy roast tomato dip.

THINK AHEAD
Make dip up to 2 days in advance. Cover and refrigerate. Marinate tuna up to 4 hours in advance. Store in an airtight container in the refrigerator. Skewer up to 2 hours in advance. Store in an airtight container in the refrigerator. Reheat dip just before serving.

COOKS' NOTE
Oven roasting tomatoes concentrates their flavor and is a very good treatment for out of season or less than ripe tomatoes.

CURRIED COCONUT CHICKEN STICKS

MAKES 20

2 boneless, skinless chicken breasts

FOR MARINADE

4 lemon grass stalks
1 tbsp curry powder
4 garlic cloves, chopped
2-inch piece fresh ginger, chopped
2 shallots, chopped
1 cup cilantro leaves
4 tbsp fish sauce
½ cup canned coconut milk
1 tsp salt, ¼ tsp black pepper
**banana leaves for serving (available in
  ethnic markets)**

ESSENTIAL EQUIPMENT
20 - 6-inch wooden skewers presoaked in cold water

Cut chicken into 20 - 1-inch cubes. For marinade, remove and discard the tough outer skin from the lemon grass stalks and finely chop. Place lemon grass, curry powder, garlic, ginger, shallots, cilantro, fish sauce, coconut milk, salt, and pepper in a food processor or blender; pulse until smooth. Toss chicken and marinade together in a nonmetallic bowl to coat each piece well. Cover and refrigerate for at least 1 hour. Thread 1 chicken cube onto each presoaked skewer. Preheat broiler. Alternatively, preheat a ridged cast-iron griddle, broiler pan, or barbecue. Broil chicken sticks until cooked through, 5 minutes on each side. Serve hot, warm or at room temperature, arranged on banana leaves.

THINK AHEAD
Marinate chicken up to 1 day in advance. Skewer chicken up to 12 hours in advance. Store in an airtight container in the refrigerator.

LEMON AND SAFFRON CHICKEN BROCHETTES

MAKES 20

2 boneless, skinless chicken breasts

FOR MARINADE

1 large pinch of saffron
½ medium onion, finely chopped
grated zest and juice of 1 lemon
4 tbsp olive oil
1 tsp salt, ½ tsp black pepper

ESSENTIAL EQUIPMENT
20 - 6-inch wooden skewers presoaked in cold water

Cut chicken into 20 - 1-inch cubes. For marinade, combine saffron, onion, lemon, oil, salt, and pepper in a nonmetallic bowl. Add chicken and toss to coat each piece well. Cover and refrigerate for at least 1 hour. Thread 1 chicken cube onto each presoaked skewer. Preheat broiler. Alternatively, preheat a ridged cast-iron griddle, broiler pan, or barbecue. Broil or grill chicken brochettes until cooked through, 5 minutes on each side. Serve hot or warm.

THINK AHEAD
Marinate chicken up to 1 day in advance. Skewer chicken up to 12 hours in advance. Store in an airtight container in the refrigerator.

COOK'S NOTE
An important reminder: don't forget to presoak wooden skewers when using them in a boiling recipe. Allow the skewers to soak for at least 30 minutes in cold water to prevent them from scorching.

THAI CHICKEN AND LEMON GRASS STICKS WITH SWEET CUCUMBER DIPPING SAUCE

MAKES 20

11 lemon grass stalks
2 boneless, skinless chicken breasts
2 garlic cloves, chopped
1 red chili, seeded and chopped
2 tbsp chopped cilantro
1 tsp brown sugar
1 tsp salt

FOR SAUCE

½ cup rice vinegar
⅔ cup sugar
2 garlic cloves, finely chopped
2 red chilies, seeded and finely chopped
½ tsp salt
¼ cucumber, seeded and finely diced
1 tbsp finely chopped cilantro

For lemon grass sticks, remove and discard the tough outer skin from the lemon grass. Set 1 stalk aside to flavor the chicken. Cut each of the 10 remaining lemon grass stalks in half lengthwise, keeping the stalks attached by the root. Trim to 5-inch lengths (see page 148). Place the reserved lemon grass stalk, chicken, garlic, chili, cilantro, sugar and salt in a food processor; pulse to a smooth paste. Divide into 20 equal-sized pieces. With wet hands, roll into oval shapes. Skewer each chicken oval on to the pointed end of a lemon grass length. Cover and refrigerate for 30 minutes to allow the flavors to blend.
For sauce, bring vinegar and sugar to a boil in a pan over medium heat. Simmer gently until syrupy, 5 minutes. Pour syrup over garlic, chilies and salt in a separate bowl and cool. Stir in cucumber and cilantro when cool. Let stand for 15 minutes at room temperature to allow the flavors to combine. Preheat broiler. Alternatively, preheat a ridged cast-iron griddle, broiler pan or barbecue. Broil chicken lemon grass sticks until cooked through, 5 minutes on each side. Serve hot, warm or at room temperature with the dipping sauce.

THINK AHEAD
Prepare and skewer chicken up to 12 hours in advance. Store in an airtight container in the refrigerator. Make sauce without cucumber and coriander up to 3 days in advance. Cover and refrigerate. Add cucumber and cilantro up to 3 hours before serving. Keep covered at room temperature.

CHICKEN, PROSCIUTTO AND SAGE SPIEDINI WITH ROAST PEPPER AIOLI

MAKES 20

FOR AIOLI

1 red pepper, quartered and seeded
1 recipe lemon aioli (see page 142)

FOR SPIEDINI

2 boneless, skinless chicken breasts
2 tbsp lemon juice
1 garlic clove, crushed

1 tsp salt
½ tsp black pepper
4 tbsp olive oil
5 prosciutto slices
20 sage leaves
4 slices day-old baguette, 1-inch thick

ESSENTIAL EQUIPMENT
20 - 6-inch wooden skewers presoaked in cold water

For aioli, grill and peel pepper quarters (see page 147). Place peeled pepper quarters in a food processor or blender; pulse to a smooth purée. Stir pepper purée into aioli. Let stand at room temperature for 15 minutes to allow the flavors to combine.
For spiedini, cut chicken into 1-inch cubes. Toss chicken together with lemon, garlic, salt, pepper and 4 tbsp oil in a nonmetallic bowl to coat each piece well. Cut each prosciutto slice into 4 strips. Place 1 sage leaf on each prosciutto strip. Top with 1 chicken cube. Wrap sage and prosciutto around chicken. Repeat with remaining chicken.
Cut baguette slices into 20 - 1-inch cubes. Thread 1 bread cube and 1 prosciutto-wrapped chicken cube on to each presoaked skewer. Brush bread with remaining oil. Preheat broiler. Alternatively, preheat a ridged cast-iron griddle, broiler pan or barbecue. Broil chicken spiedini until cooked through, 5 minutes on each side. Serve warm or at room temperature with roast pepper aioli.

THINK AHEAD
Make aioli up to 3 days in advance. Cover and refrigerate. Skewer chicken up to 12 hours in advance. Store in an airtight container in the refrigerator.

CHICKEN YAKITORI

MAKES 20

¾ lb boneless, skinless chicken thighs

FOR MARINADE

4 tbsp shoyu (japanese soy sauce)

2 tbsp mirin

1½ tbsp sake

1 tsp sugar

5 shiitake mushrooms

2 scallions

ESSENTIAL EQUIPMENT

20 - 6-inch wooden skewers presoaked in cold water

Cut chicken into 20 - 1-inch pieces. For marinade, place soy, mirin, sake and sugar in a small pan. Bring to a boil over medium heat. Simmer gently until slightly syrupy, 5 minutes. Cool. Toss marinade and chicken together in a non-metallic bowl to coat each piece well. Cover and refrigerate for at least 30 minutes. Cut mushrooms into quarters. Cut scallions in 20 - 1-inch lengths. Thread 1 scallion piece, 1 chicken cube and 1 mushroom quarter on to each presoaked skewer. Preheat broiler. Alternatively, preheat a ridged cast-iron griddle, broiler pan or barbecue. Broil chicken yakitori until cooked through, 5 minutes on each side. Serve hot.

THINK AHEAD
Marinate chicken up to 3 hours in advance. Assemble skewers up to 1 hour in advance. Store in an airtight container in the refrigerator.

LIME MARINATED CHICKEN SKEWERS WITH AVOCADO CREMA DIP

MAKES 20

2 boneless, skinless chicken breasts

FOR MARINADE

juice of 1 lime

1 tbsp honey

2 tbsp olive oil

2 green chilies, seeded and finely chopped

¼ cup cilantro, finely chopped

1tsp salt, ¼ tsp black pepper

ESSENTIAL EQUIPMENT

20 - 6-inch wooden skewers presoaked in cold water

FOR DIP

1 avocado, stoned

3 scallions, chopped

1 tbsp red wine vinegar

1 tbsp olive oil

½ cup sour cream

salt, black pepper

1 tbsp finely chopped cilantro to garnish

Cut chicken into 1-inch cubes.
For marinade, combine lime, honey, oil, chilies, cilantro, salt and pepper in a nonmetallic bowl. Add chicken and toss to coat each piece well. Cover and refrigerate for at least 1 hour.
For dip, place avocado, scallions, vinegar, olive oil and sour cream in a food processor or blender; pulse until smooth. Add salt and pepper to taste. Cover and refrigerate for 30 minutes to allow the flavors to blend.
Thread a chicken cube on to each presoaked skewer. Preheat broiler. Alternatively, preheat a ridged cast-iron griddle, broiler pan or barbecue. Broil chicken skewers until cooked through, 5 minutes on each side. Garnish each skewer with a sprinkling of cilantro. Serve warm with avocado crema dip.

THINK AHEAD
Marinate chicken up to 1 day in advance. Skewer chicken up to 12 hours in advance. Store in an airtight container in the refrigerator. Make dip up to 8 hours in advance.
Cover and refrigerate.

COOKS' NOTE
To prevent the avocado crema dip from discoloring when making ahead, make sure you press a piece of cling wrap directly on to the surface of the dip. It's the oxygen in the air that turns avocado brown, so the less air that comes into contact with the dip, the better.

SPICY SATAY STICKS

MAKES 20

2 boneless, skinless chicken breasts

FOR MARINADE

1 lemon grass stalk
2 shallots
2 garlic cloves
½-inch piece fresh ginger
2 tsp brown sugar
½ tsp ground cumin
½ tsp ground coriander
1 tsp turmeric
1 tsp salt
1 tbsp sunflower oil

ESSENTIAL EQUIPMENT
20 - 6-inch wooden skewers presoaked in cold water

FOR SAUCE

4 tbsp roasted peanuts
2 lemon grass stalks
2 shallots
2 garlic cloves
1-inch piece fresh ginger
1 tsp turmeric
1 tbsp sunflower oil
1 tbsp brown sugar
1 tsp fish sauce
1 tbsp Chinese hot chili sauce
juice of 1 lime
4 tbsp water
½ cup canned coconut milk

Slice chicken into 20 strips about ¼ inch thick and 2½ inches long.

For marinade, remove and discard the tough outer skin from the lemon grass and finely chop. Place lemon grass, shallots, garlic, ginger, sugar, spices, salt, and oil in a food processor or blender; pulse to a smooth paste. Toss chicken and marinade together in a nonmetallic bowl to coat each piece well. Cover and refrigerate for at least 1 hour.

For sauce, place peanuts in a food processor or blender; pulse until finely ground. Set aside. Remove and discard the tough outer skin from the lemon grass and finely chop. Place shallots, garlic, ginger, chopped lemon grass, turmeric, and sunflower oil in a food processor or blender; pulse to a smooth paste. Heat a frying pan over a medium heat. Add paste and stir fry until softened, 5 minutes. Stir in ground peanuts, sugar, fish sauce, chili sauce, lime, water, and coconut milk. Cook, stirring occasionally, until the sauce thickens, 10 minutes. Keep warm.

Thread 1 chicken strip onto each presoaked skewer, running the skewer through it like a ruffled ribbon. Preheat broiler. Alternatively, preheat a ridged cast-iron griddle, broiler pan, or barbecue. Broil or grill chicken satay sticks until cooked through, 5 minutes on each side. Serve hot with warm satay sauce.

THINK AHEAD
Make sauce up 4 days in advance. Cover and refrigerate. Marinate chicken up to 1 day in advance. Skewer chicken up to 12 hours in advance. Store in an airtight container in the refrigerator. Reheat sauce before serving.

COOKS' NOTE
The satay sauce will thicken on standing, so, if making ahead, keep in mind that you may need to thin it with a tablespoon or so of lime juice when you reheat.

CUMIN SCENTED KOFTE BROCHETTES WITH MINTED YOGURT DIP

MAKES 20

¾ lb lean ground lamb
1 medium onion, grated
2 garlic cloves, chopped
2 tsp ground cumin
½ tsp ground coriander
grated zest of 1 lemon
2 tbsp finely chopped cilantro leaves
1½ tsp salt
¼ tsp cayenne pepper

FOR DIP

¾ cup whole-milk yogurt
¼ cup mint leaves, finely chopped
¼ cup parsley leaves, finely chopped
juice of ½ lemon
salt, cayenne pepper

ESSENTIAL EQUIPMENT
20 - 6-inch wooden skewers presoaked in cold water

Place lamb, onion, garlic, cumin, ground coriander, lemon zest, fresh cilantro, salt, and cayenne pepper in a food processor; pulse until combined and slightly pasty. Divide into 20 equal-sized pieces. With wet hands, roll into oval shapes. Thread 1 oval onto each presoaked skewer. Cover and refrigerate for 30 minutes.
For dip, combine yogurt, mint, parsley, and lemon juice. Add salt and cayenne pepper to taste. Cover and refrigerate for 30 minutes to allow the flavors to blend.
Preheat broiler. Alternatively, preheat a ridged cast-iron griddle, broiler pan, or barbecue. Broil or grill brochettes until browned but still pink and juicy inside, 3 minutes on each side. Serve hot with chilled minted yogurt dip.

THINK AHEAD
Make dip up to 1 day in advance. Cover and refrigerate. Prepare and skewer kofte up to 12 hours in advance. Store in an airtight container in the refrigerator.

SESAME SOY GLAZED BEEF SKEWERS

MAKES 20

¾ lb beef fillet or sirloin, 1 inch thick
4 scallions, white stalk only
1 red pepper, halved and seeded

FOR GLAZE

2 tbsp sesame seeds
2 lemon grass stalks, tender interior stalk only, finely chopped
1 tbsp honey
2 tbsp sesame oil
1 tbsp sunflower oil
2 tbsp light soy sauce
1 tbsp Chinese hot chili sauce
½ tsp black pepper
1 tsp salt

ESSENTIAL EQUIPMENT
20 - 6-inch wooden skewers presoaked in cold water

Cut beef into 20 - 1-inch cubes. Cut scallions diagonally into 20 - 1-inch pieces.
Cut pepper into 20   1 inch pieces.
For glaze, combine seeds, lemon grass, honey, oils, soy sauce, chili sauce, black pepper, and salt in a nonmetallic bowl. Add beef, scallions, and peppers. Toss to coat each piece well. Cover and refrigerate for at least 1 hour.
Thread 1 piece each of scallion and pepper and 1 beef cube onto each presoaked skewer.
Preheat broiler. Alternatively, preheat ridged cast-iron griddle, broiler pan, or barbecue. Broil or grill beef skewers until browned but still pink and juicy inside, 3 minutes on each side. Serve hot.

THINK AHEAD
Marinate beef up to 1 day in advance. Store in an airtight container in the refrigerator. Skewer beef up to 12 hours in advance. Store in an airtight container in the refrigerator.

MINT MARINATED LAMB KEBABS WITH TAHINI AND HONEY DIP

MAKES 20

¾ lb lean boneless lamb

FOR MARINADE

½ cup mint leaves, finely chopped
2 garlic cloves, crushed
1 tbsp honey
2 tbsp lemon juice
2 tbsp olive oil
1 tsp salt
½ tsp pepper

FOR DIP

2 tbsp sesame seeds
2 tsp honey
juice of 1 lemon
5 tbsp tahini
½ cup whole-milk yogurt
3 tbsp water
salt, black pepper

ESSENTIAL EQUIPMENT
20 - 6-inch wooden skewers presoaked in cold water

Cut lamb into 20 - 1-inch cubes.
For marinade, combine half of the chopped mint, garlic, honey, lemon juice, oil, salt, and pepper. Add lamb and toss to coat each piece well. Cover and refrigerate. Let marinate for at least 1 hour.
For dip, toast seeds in a dry pan over low heat until nutty and golden, 3 minutes. Combine seeds, honey, lemon juice, tahini, yogurt, and water. Add salt and pepper to taste. Cover and refrigerate. Leave for 30 minutes for the flavors to blend. Thread 1 lamb cube on to each presoaked skewer. Preheat broiler. Alternatively, preheat ridged cast-iron griddle, broiler pan, or barbecue. Broil lamb kebabs until browned but still pink and juicy inside, 3 minutes on each side. Garnish each kebab with a sprinkling of the remaining mint. Serve hot with chilled tahini and honey dip.

THINK AHEAD
Make dip up to 2 days in advance. Cover and refrigerate. Marinate lamb up to 1 day in advance. Skewer lamb up to 12 hours in advance. Store in an airtight container in the refrigerator.

GINGER ORANGE PORK SKEWERS

MAKES 20

¾ lb lean boneless pork

FOR MARINADE

2-inch piece fresh ginger, grated
grated zest of 1 orange
juice of ½ orange
2 tsp Dijon mustard
2 tsp honey

1 tbsp balsamic vinegar
2 tbsp light soy sauce
4 tbsp olive oil
1 tsp salt
½ tsp black pepper
2-inch piece fresh ginger for garnish

ESSENTIAL EQUIPMENT
20 - 6-inch wooden skewers presoaked in cold water

Cut pork into 20 - 1-inch cubes. Combine grated ginger, orange juice and zest, mustard, honey, vinegar, soy, oil, salt, and pepper in a nonmetallic bowl. Add pork and toss to coat each piece well. Cover and refrigerate for at least 1 hour. For garnish, preheat oven to 400°F. Cut ginger piece for garnish into fine slices. Cut ginger slices into julienne (see page 147). Bring a pan of water to a boil over high heat. Add ginger julienne and boil for 1 minute. Drain. Spread ginger julienne in a single layer on a baking sheet. Bake until crispy and dry, 5–10 minutes. Cool.
Preheat broiler. Alternatively, preheat ridged cast-iron griddle, broiler pan, or barbecue. Broil or grill pork skewers until cooked through, 5 minutes on each side. Sprinkle each skewer with crisp ginger garnish. Serve hot.

THINK AHEAD
Make crisp ginger garnish up to 2 days in advance. Store in an airtight container at room temperature. Marinate pork up to 1 day in advance. Store in an airtight container in the refrigerator. Skewer pork up to 12 hours in advance. Store in an airtight container in the refrigerator.

TROPICAL FRUIT BROCHETTES WITH PASSION FRUIT AND MASCARPONE DIP

MAKES 20

1 firm mango, peeled and pit removed
2 firm kiwi, peeled
¼ watermelon, rind removed

FOR DIP

2 passion fruit, halved
1 cup mascarpone cheese
1 tbsp honey
1 tbsp grated orange zest

ESSENTIAL EQUIPMENT
20 wooden toothpicks

Cut each fruit into 20 - ¾-inch cubes. Thread 3 different fruit cubes onto each skewer. Cover and refrigerate for 30 minutes.
For dip, spoon passion fruit pulp out from the center of each half with a teaspoon. Strain pulp and discard seeds. Combine passion fruit pulp, mascarpone, honey, and zest. Cover and refrigerate for 30 minutes. Serve chilled tropical fruit brochettes with chilled passion fruit and mascarpone dip.

THINK AHEAD
Make dip up to 1 day in advance. Cover and refrigerate. Skewer fruit up to 4 hours in advance. Cover and refrigerate.

COOKS' NOTE
These brochettes are open to variation. Use your favorite combination of tropical fruit. For the prettiest brochettes, think about complimentary colors as well as flavors. Try to select firm, just ripe fruits that will cube and skewer easily.

PROSCIUTTO-WRAPPED FIG SKEWERS

MAKES 20

10 very thin prosciutto slices
4 oz piece Parmesan cheese
5 ripe figs, quartered
black pepper
½ tbsp grated Parmesan cheese

ESSENTIAL EQUIPMENT
vegetable peeler
20 - 6-inch wooden skewers

Cut each prosciutto slice lengthwise into 2 strips. Shave the Parmesan with a vegetable peeler to make 20 shavings (see page 148). Place 1 Parmesan shaving on each prosciutto strip. Place 1 fig quarter on top. Sprinkle with a pinch of pepper. Wrap up the fig in prosciutto. Secure with skewer. Sprinkle with grated Parmesan just before serving. Serve chilled or at room temperature.

THINK AHEAD
Skewer figs up to 4 hours in advance. Cover and refrigerate.

COOKS' NOTE
Firm melon and papaya slices make good substitutes when figs are not in season. Speck, coppa, or serrano are a few of the huge wealth of cured hams that are suitable alternatives to prosciutto. To make wrapping easy, make sure any ham you choose is sliced very thin.

CHERUBS ON HORSEBACK

MAKES 20

20 dried apricots, soaked in hot water for 10 minutes and drained
10 slices of bacon

ESSENTIAL EQUIPMENT
20 wooden toothpicks presoaked in cold water

Preheat oven 400°F.
Cut the bacon in half crosswise. Stretch each piece of bacon by running the back of a knife along the bacon slice. This will help prevent shrinking during cooking. Wrap 1 bacon piece around each apricot. Secure with a presoaked skewer. Place skewered apricots on a baking pan. Bake until bacon is crisp, 10 minutes. Serve hot or warm.

THINK AHEAD
Wrap and skewer apricots up to 1 day in advance. Store in an airtight container in the refrigerator.

BASIL MARINATED MOZZARELLA AND CHERRY TOMATO SKEWERS

MAKES 20

1 red pepper, quartered and seeded
1 garlic clove, finely chopped
1 tbsp lemon juice
2 tbsp olive oil
½ tsp salt
1 tsp cracked black pepper
20 bocconcini (baby mozzarella balls)
1/4 cup finely chopped basil
20 cherry tomatoes, halved
20 large basil leaves

ESSENTIAL EQUIPMENT
20 - 6-inch wooden skewers

LEMON MARINATED TORTELLINI AND SUN-DRIED TOMATO SKEWERS

MAKES 20

20 fresh spinach and ricotta tortellini
10 sun-dried tomatoes in oil,
  drained and halved
20 large basil leaves

FOR MARINADE
1 tsp grated lemon zest
2 tbsp lemon juice
4 tbsp olive oil
salt, black pepper

ESSENTIAL EQUIPMENT
20 - 6-inch wooden skewers

Cook tortellini in salted boiling water until tender, 4 minutes, or according to instructions on the package. Drain and rinse with cold water. Spread out in a single layer on a clean tea towel to dry. For marinade, whisk lemon and oil until thick and combined. Toss the cooled pasta and marinade together in a nonmetallic bowl to coat each piece well. Add salt and pepper to taste. Cover and marinate at room temperature for 30 minutes. Thread 1 tortellini and 1 sun-dried tomato half wrapped in 1 basil leaf onto each skewer. Serve at room temperature.

THINK AHEAD
Marinate tortellini up to 1 day in advance. Cover and refrigerate. Assemble skewers up to 4 hours in advance. Return to room temperature before serving.

Grill and peel pepper quarters (see page 147). Cut pepper quarters into very fine dice (see page 147). Combine pepper dice, garlic, lemon, oil, salt, and cracked pepper in a nonmetallic bowl. Add bocconcini and toss to coat each piece well. Cover and marinate at room temperature for at least 30 minutes. Sprinkle basil over and toss to coat each bocconcini well. Thread 1 cherry tomato half and 1 bocconcini on to each skewer. Wrap each remaining cherry tomato half in 1 basil leaf and add 1 to each skewer. Serve chilled or at room temperature.

THINK AHEAD
Marinate bocconcini up to 3 days in advance. Store in an airtight container in the refrigerator. Assemble skewers up to 4 hours in advance. Cover and refrigerate.

COOKS' NOTE
Bocconcini means "mouthful" in Italian. If you can't find these baby mozzarella balls, cut whole mozzarella cheese (you'll need 1 large one) into 20 - ¾-inch cubes, then marinate and skewer as directed.

FENNEL MARINATED FETA AND OLIVE SKEWERS

MAKES 20

2 tbsp sesame seeds
½ lb feta cheese
1 tbsp fennel seeds
grated zest of 1 lemon
1 tbsp lemon juice
2 tbsp olive oil
1½ tsp cracked black pepper
¼ cup finely chopped mint leaves
20 mint leaves
½ cucumber, peeled and seeded
10 pitted black olives, halved

ESSENTIAL EQUIPMENT
20 - 6-inch wooden skewers

Toast seeds in a dry pan over low heat until nutty and golden, 3 minutes. Cool. Gently rinse feta in cold water. Drain on paper towels. Cut feta into 2¾-inch cubes. Toss feta together with fennel, toasted sesame seeds, lemon, oil, and pepper to coat each cube well. Cover and refrigerate for 4 hours to allow the flavors to combine. Sprinkle feta with chopped mint and toss to coat each cube well. Cut cucumber into 20 - ½-inch cubes. Thread 1 mint leaf, 1 olive half, 1 cucumber cube, and 1 feta cube on to each skewer. Serve chilled or at room temperature.

THINK AHEAD
Marinate feta up to 3 days in advance. Store in an airtight container in the refrigerator. Skewer feta up to 4 hours in advance. Cover and refrigerate.

HAM AND DIJON MINI CROISSANTS

MAKES 20

1 sheet puff pastry
3 tbsp Dijon mustard
¼ lb ham slices
1 egg yolk beaten with 1 tbsp water

Preheat oven to 400°F.
Roll out pastry to a 7 x 18-inch rectangle. Trim uneven edges with a sharp knife. Cut pastry in half lengthwise to make 2 strips each 3½ inches wide. Cut each strip diagonally into 10 even-sized triangles (see below, left). Cut ham into strips about 4 inches long and ¼-inch wide. Spread each pastry triangle with mustard. Place ham on longest edge. Roll up each triangle, starting at the long edge and ending with the point (see below, right). Place on an oiled baking sheet. Curl ends in to make a crescent. Tuck the points underneath to prevent the croissants from unraveling as they bake. Brush croissants with beaten egg. Bake until crisp and golden, 10 minutes. Cool on wire rack. Serve warm or at room temperature.

THINK AHEAD
Bake up to 3 days in advance. Store in an airtight container at room temperature. Crisp in preheated 400°F oven, 3 minutes.

SMOKED SALMON RUGALACH

MAKES 32

FOR PASTRY
½ cup cream cheese
6 tbsp cold butter, diced
1 cup all-purpose flour
pinch salt

FOR FILLING
½ lb smoked salmon slices
1 tbsp lemon juice
¼ tsp black pepper
1 tbsp finely chopped fresh dill
1 egg yolk beaten with 1 tbsp water

Preheat oven to 400°F.
Place cream cheese, butter, flour, and salt in a food processor; pulse until smooth dough forms. Refrigerate 30 minutes. Divide pastry into 2 equal-sized pieces. Roll out each piece to a 9-inch round. Cover each round with a single layer of smoked salmon slices. Cut each round crosswise into 16 even-sized triangles. Sprinkle with lemon juice, pepper, and dill. Roll up each triangle, starting at the long edge and ending with the point. Place on an oiled baking sheet. Curl ends in to make a crescent. Tuck the points underneath to prevent the rugalach from unraveling as they bake. Refrigerate until firm, 20 minutes. Brush rugalach with beaten egg. ake until crisp and golden, 10 minutes. Cool on wire rack. Serve warm.

THINK AHEAD
Bake up to 3 days in advance. Store in an airtight container at room temperature. Crisp in preheated 400°F oven, 3 minutes.

QUEEN OLIVE CHEESE BALLS

MAKES 20

20 pitted large green olives
1 cup grated Parmesan cheese
4 tbsp cold butter, diced
¾ cup all-purpose flour
salt, cayenne pepper
1 egg yolk beaten with 1 tbsp water
1 tsp poppy seeds

Preheat oven 350°F.
Pat olives dry with paper towels. Place Parmesan, butter, and flour with pinch each salt and cayenne pepper in a food processor; pulse until smooth pastry forms. Divide pastry into 20 equal-sized pieces. With floured hands, press 1 piece of pastry around each olive to enclose completely. Roll pastry-wrapped olives between palms of your hands to make smooth, olive shapes. Place on an oiled baking sheet. Refrigerate until firm, 30 minutes. Brush pastry with beaten egg. Sprinkle with seeds. Bake until golden, 20 minutes. Cool on a wire rack. Serve warm or at room temperature.

THINK AHEAD
Bake up to 3 days in advance. Store in an airtight container at room temperature. Crisp in preheated 400°F oven, 3 minutes.

COOKS' NOTE
If you can't find pitted large green olives, use 30 regular pitted olives instead.

Mark the triangle shapes with the back of a knife before cutting.

SPICY PORK EMPANADITAS WITH CHUNKY AVOCADO RELISH

MAKES 20

FOR FILLING

1 tbsp sunflower oil
½ medium onion, finely chopped
¾ lb ground pork
3 garlic cloves, finely chopped
1 red chili, seeded and
  finely chopped
½ tsp ground cumin
¼ tsp ground cinnamon
pinch of ground cloves
½ cup tomato juice
1 tsp tomato purée
2 tbsp raisins
10 pimento-stuffed green olives,
  chopped
salt, black pepper

FOR PASTRY

1½ cups all-purpose flour
½ tsp salt
2 tbsp butter
⅛ cup warm water

ESSENTIAL EQUIPMENT

1 - 2¼ -inch plain pastry cutter

FOR RELISH

½ medium onion, finely
  chopped
2 red chilies, seeded and
  finely chopped
2 tomatoes, peeled, seeded
  and finely chopped
  (see page 147)
1 garlic clove, finely chopped
2 tbsp finely chopped
  cilantro leaves
juice of 1 lime
2 medium avocados, peeled
  and pitted
salt

For filling, heat oil in a frying pan over medium heat.
Stir fry onions in oil until soft, 5 minutes. Add pork. Stir pork
constantly with a fork to break up any lumps, until lightly
browned, 5 minutes. Add garlic and chilies and cook until
fragrant, 3 minutes. Add spices, tomato juice, tomato purée,
raisins, and olives. Reduce heat to low and simmer, stirring
occasionally, until thick, 15 minutes. Cool. Add salt and
pepper to taste. Cover and refrigerate until chilled, 30 minutes.
For pastry, sift flour and salt into a bowl. Rub butter into the
flour with fingers until mixture resembles fine crumbs. Use a
fork to stir in the water to make a firm dough. Turn dough
onto a lightly floured surface and knead until smooth,
3 minutes. Wrap dough in plastic wrap and let rest at room
temperature for 30 minutes. Roll out dough to a ⅛-inch
thickness. Cut out 20 rounds with the pastry cutter. Place 1 tsp
of filling in center of each round. Fold pastry over filling to
make crescents. Pinch edges firmly together to seal. With
fingertips, seal edges (see opposite).
Place empanaditas on oiled baking sheets. Brush with
beaten egg. Bake until crisp and golden, 15 minutes. Cool on
a wire rack.
For relish, combine onion, chili, tomato, garlic, cilantro, and
lime. Cut avocados into 1-inch cubes. Mash the avocado into
the onion mixture while combining with the other
ingredients. Add salt to taste. Cover plastic wrap tightly over
the surface of the relish. Refrigerate for 15 minutes.
Serve empanaditas warm or at room temperature with relish
for dipping.

EMPANADITAS FILLING VARIATIONS

SPICY CHORIZO EMPANADITAS

Use ⅓ lb crumbled chorizo sausage instead of ground pork
when making the filling.

HOT PEPPER AND SMOKY MOZZARELLA EMPANADITAS

Make hot pepper relish (see page 119). Fill pastry rounds with
1 tsp grated smoked mozzarella and 1 tsp relish instead of
spicy pork mixture.

THINK AHEAD

Assemble empanaditas up to 1 day in advance. Cover and refrigerate. Bake
empanaditas up to 8 hours in advance. Keep at room temperature. Make relish
up to 3 hours in advance. Cover tightly with plastic wrap and refrigerate.

COOKS' NOTE

The secret to juicy empanaditas is to chill the filling before assembling. The juices
in the filling will solidify so that the empanaditas won't leak as they are assembled.
Press a piece of plastic wrap directly on to the surface of the relish to keep out
the air that causes the avocado to darken. If the relish does discolor slightly,
simply scrape off the dark surface. The relish will still be green underneath.

FRESH HERB AND SHRIMP RICE PAPER ROLLS WITH PEANUT-HOISIN DIPPING SAUCE

MAKES 20

1 carrot, cut into julienne strips (see page 147)
1 tsp sugar
10 medium shrimp, cooked and peeled
5 small lettuce leaves
1 cup cilantro leaves
10 sheets of rice paper
20 mint leaves

FOR SAUCE

2 tbsp hoisin sauce
2 tbsp smooth peanut butter
1 tbsp tomato ketchup
5 tbsp water

Combine carrot strips with sugar and toss to coat each piece well. Let stand until wilted, 15 minutes.

Cut shrimp in half lengthwise. Cut lettuce leaves into 2 x 1-inch strips. Divide carrots and cilantro into 20 equal-sized portions. Set aside.

Pour about ¾-inch cold water into a shallow dish. Dip 1 sheet of rice paper into the water and let soften, 2 minutes. Remove and spread out on a dry dish towel. Cut in half.

Top 1 half sheet with 1 lettuce strip, 1 mint leaf and 1 portion each of carrots and cilantro. Fold both ends of rice paper over the enclosed filling. Place 1 shrimp half, cut side down, on top (see below, left). Roll up into a cylinder and press the end with a wet finger to seal. Place the roll, seal side down, on a tray and cover with a dampened dish towel to keep moist. Repeat with the remaining half sheet rice paper, then start again with remaining rice paper sheets and filling.

For sauce, combine hoisin, peanut butter, ketchup, and water. Serve rice paper rolls chilled or at room temperature with peanut-hoisin dipping sauce.

THINK AHEAD
Prepare filling ingredients up to 1 day in advance. Cover and refrigerate. Make rolls up to 3 hours in advance. Cover with a dampened dish towel and refrigerate. Be sure to keep the dish towel moist.

CRAB AND PAPAYA RICE PAPER ROLLS WITH SWEET CHILI DIPPING SAUCE

MAKES 20

¼ lb crab meat
2 scallions, cut into julienne strips (see page 147)
½ cucumber, seeded and cut into julienne strips (see page 147)
10 sheets of rice paper
1 papaya, peeled, quartered, and finely sliced
20 mint leaves
20 basil leaves

FOR SAUCE

2 tbsp sugar
2 tbsp boiling water
2 tbsp fish sauce
2 tbsp lime juice
1 tbsp rice vinegar
1 red chili, seeded and chopped
1 garlic, crushed

Divide the crab, scallions, and cucumber strips into 20 equal-sized portions.

Pour about ¾-inch cold water into a shallow dish. Dip 1 sheet of rice paper into the water and leave to soften, 2 minutes. Remove and spread out on a dry dish towel. Cut in half. Top 1 half with 1 portion of crab, scallion, and cucumber. Place 1 papaya slice, 1 mint leaf, and 1 basil leaf on top of the cucumber so that they stick out slightly over the straight end of the rice paper. Roll rice paper over to enclose filling. Fold one end of the rice paper over the enclosed filling to make a 2-inch cylinder. Continue rolling up into a cylinder and press the end with a wet finger to seal. Place the roll, seal side down on a tray and cover with a dampened dish towel to keep moist. Repeat with the remaining half sheet rice paper, then start again with remaining rice paper sheets and filling.

For sauce, dissolve sugar in boiling water. Combine dissolved sugar, fish sauce, lime, vinegar, chili, and garlic.

Serve rice paper rolls chilled or at room temperature with sweet chili dipping sauce.

THINK AHEAD
Prepare filling ingredients up to 1 day in advance. Cover and refrigerate. Make rolls up to 3 hours in advance. Cover with a dampened dish towel and refrigerate. Be sure to keep the kitchen dish moist.

COOKS' NOTE
Rice paper is fragile and tricky to work with. Be prepared to discard some rice papers if they tear and have extra rice papers in reserve to replace them.

Enclose shrimp in rice paper.

SUSHI RICE

MAKES 2 CUPS

1 cup short-grained rice
1 cup water
½ cup rice vinegar
5 tbsp sugar

Put rice in a large bowl. Cover with cold tap water and stir with your fingers until water turns cloudy. Pour off water. Repeat this 1 or 2 more times until water is almost clear. Drain rice in a strainer. Put drained rice in a pan, add 1 cup water, cover, and bring to a boil over high heat. Boil for 2 minutes. Reduce heat to low and simmer until water is absorbed and rice is tender, 15 minutes. Remove from heat and let stand without lifting the lid, for 5 minutes.

In separate pan, bring vinegar and sugar to boil over medium heat, stirring until the sugar dissolves. Remove from heat and cool. Turn the hot cooked rice out onto an baking sheet and immediately drizzle the vinegar and sugar mixture evenly over the rice. Toss gently but thoroughly with a wooden spoon. Quickly cool the rice to room temperature by fanning it while continuing to toss the rice. Cover the rice with a dampened dish towel and cool completely.

THINK AHEAD
Make rice up to 3 hours in advance. Store covered with a dampened dishtowel at room temperature.

COOKS' NOTE
Fanning the rice as it cools will make the rice especially glossy. Use a piece of stiff cardboard or a baking sheet if you don't have a fan.

CUCUMBER NORI SUSHI ROLLS

MAKES 24

2 tsp sesame seeds
2 sheets of nori, halved
1 recipe sushi rice (see left)
½ tsp wasabi paste
½ cucumber, seeded and cut into julienne strips (see page 147)
2 tbsp pickled ginger
6 tbsp shoyu (Japanese soy sauce)

ESSENTIAL EQUIPMENT
bamboo sushi mat

Toast seeds in a dry pan over low heat until nutty and golden, 3 minutes. Cool. Have a small bowl of water ready for moistening your fingers. Place ½-piece nori, smooth-side down, on the mat. Moisten your fingers with water, then spread ¼ of the rice in an even layer on the nori, leaving a ½-inch strip uncovered at the far end. Press down on the rice with moistened fingers to pack firmly. Spread a thin line of wasabi lengthwise along the center of the rice with your finger. Arrange ¼ of the cucumber, sesame seeds, and ginger on top, making sure the fillings extend completely to each end of the rice. Pick up the bamboo mat and tightly roll rice around the filling, pulling the mat as you roll (see right). Unroll mat. Repeat with remaining ingredients. Cut each nori roll into 6 equal-sized pieces with a moist knife. Serve chilled or at room temperature with soy sauce for dipping.

THINK AHEAD
Make but do not cut nori rolls up to 1 day in advance. Store wrapped in plastic wrap at room temperature.

SMOKED SALMON SUSHI RICE BALLS

MAKES 20

¼ lb smoked salmon slices
1 recipe sushi rice (see far left)
1 tsp wasabi paste

Cut salmon into 20 - 1-inch squares. Divide the rice into 20 equal-sized portions. Cut the plastic wrap into 20 - 4-inch squares. Place 1 piece of salmon in the center of 1 plastic wrap square. Place 1 portion of rice on top. Gather plastic wrap around the rice and twist the ends to make a tight ball (see below, right). Repeat with remaining salmon, plastic wrap, and rice. Unwrap rice balls. Garnish with a knife's tip of wasabi. Serve chilled or at room temperature

THINK AHEAD
Make rice balls up to 2 days in advance. Refrigerate wrapped. Garnish up to 1 hour before serving.

SUSHI RICE BALL VARIATIONS

SALMON CAVIAR SUSHI RICE BALLS

Omit smoked salmon. Replace wasabi garnish with 6 tbsp salmon caviar. Wrap rice in plastic wrap as directed to make rice balls. Garnish each rice ball with 1 tsp salmon caviar up to 1 hour before serving.

SHRIMP SUSHI RICE BALLS

Substitute smoked salmon with 10 cooked, peeled medium shrimp cut in half lengthwise. Place 1 shrimp half cut side up on each piece of plastic wrap. Top with rice and wrap in plastic wrap as directed to make rice balls. Garnish with wasabi as directed.

THINK AHEAD
Make rice balls up to 2 days in advance. Refrigerate wrapped. Garnish up to 1 hour before serving.

Pull mat as you roll.   Twist to make tight balls.

MINI CALIFORNIA ROLLS

MAKES 40

5 sheets of nori
1 recipe sushi rice (see page 89)
½ cucumber, seeded and cut into julienne strips (see page 147)
1 avocado, peeled, pitted, and finely sliced into 40 pieces
40 pickled ginger slices
1 tsp wasabi

ESSENTIAL EQUIPMENT
bamboo sushi mat

Fold nori sheets into three, lengthwise, to make a strip. Fold the strip into thirds. Unfold and tear along the folded lines to make squares. Place the squares smooth side down. Have a small bowl of water ready for moistening your fingers. Place 1 half, smooth side down, on the mat. Divide the rice and cucumber into 40 equal-sized portions. Moisten your fingers with water, then spread 1 rice portion in an even layer over the left half of 1 nori square. Spread a thin line of wasabi lengthwise along the center of the rice with your finger. Arrange 1 portion cucumber, 1 avocado slice and 1 ginger piece on top. Starting at the left corner, roll up the nori square like a cone, moistening with a wet finger to stick the nori together (see below, left). Repeat with remaining nori, rice, wasabi, cucumber, avocado, and ginger. Serve at room temperature.

THINK AHEAD
Assemble up to 1 hour in advance. Cover with plastic wrap and store at room temperature.

SESAME SUSHI ROLLS

MAKES 24

3 tbsp sesame seeds, white and black
¼ lb medium shrimp
2 sheets of nori, halved
1 recipe sushi rice (see page 89)
½ tsp wasabi paste
½ cucumber, seeded and cut into julienne strips (see page 147)
6 tbsp shoyu (Japanese soy sauce)

ESSENTIAL EQUIPMENT
bamboo sushi mat

Toast seeds in a dry pan over low heat until nutty and golden, 3 minutes. Cool. Cut shrimp in half lengthwise.
Have a small bowl of water ready for moistening your fingers. Cut 1 sheet of plastic wrap just larger than 1 nori half. Place 1 nori half, smooth side down, on the mat. Moisten your fingers with water, then spread a quarter of the rice in an even layer on the nori. Cover with the plastic wrap. Pick up the nori, carefully turn over and place on the mat plastic wrap side down. The nori should now be facing up. Spread a thin line of wasabi lengthwise along the center of the nori with your finger. Arrange a quarter of the shrimp, cucumber, and 1 tsp sesame seeds on top, making sure the fillings extend completely to each end. Pick up the bamboo mat and plastic wrap and tightly roll rice around the filling, pressing down firmly as you roll. Unroll mat and plastic wrap. Gently roll the rice roll in half the remaining sesame seeds (see bottom left, center). Roll up tightly in plastic wrap, twisting the ends to secure (see bottom left, right). Repeat with remaining nori, rice, wasabi, shrimp, cucumber, and sesame seeds. Trim the ends of each roll to neaten, then cut each rice roll into 6 equal-sized pieces with a moist knife. Remove plastic wrap from the cut pieces. Serve at room temperature with shoyu for dipping.

THINK AHEAD
Assemble but do not cut rice rolls up to 1 day in advance. Store wrapped in plastic wrap at room temperature. Cut when ready to serve.

COOKS' NOTE
We used a mixture of black and brown sesame seeds for coating the roll that is pictured here. For an alternative coating, try 2 tbsp red lumpfish roe.

WONTON WRAPPERS

MAKES 20

1¼ cups all-purpose flour
½ cup boiling water

ESSENTIAL EQUIPMENT
2-inch plain pastry cutter

Place the flour in a bowl and make a well in the center. Pour in the water. Mix with a fork to form a rough dough. Cover with a dish towel and let stand until cool enough to handle. Knead on a lightly floured surface until smooth and elastic, 5 minutes. Cover with a dish towel and let rest for 30 minutes. Roll out dough on a lightly floured surface to a ⅛-inch thickness. Cut out 20 rounds with the pastry cutter.

THINK AHEAD
Make up to 1 day in advance. Store in an airtight container stacked in single layers separated by waxed paper. Alternatively, freeze wrappers up to 1 month in advance. Store in a sealed plastic freezer bag stacked in single layers separated by plastic wrap (see page 149). Defrost overnight in the refrigerator.

CRISPY WONTON CRESCENTS WITH GINGERED PORK AND CHILI SOY DIPPING SAUCE

MAKES 20

2½ oz lean ground pork
1 garlic clove, crushed
1 scallion, chopped
¾-inch piece ginger, grated
1 tbsp dark soy sauce
1 tsp sesame oil
1 recipe wonton wrappers, or 20 store-bought round dumpling wrappers
2 tbsp all-purpose flour for dusting
2 tbsp sunflower oil
1 cup cold water for cooking

FOR SAUCE
1 tbsp chinese hot chili sauce
4 tbsp dark soy sauce

ESSENTIAL EQUIPMENT
wok with a lid

Place pork, garlic, scallion, ginger, soy sauce, and sesame oil in a food processor or blender; pulse until well combined. Place ⅛ tsp pork filling in the center of each wrapper. Fold wrapper over to enclose filling to make crescents. Press edges together to seal. With fingertips, crimp edges (see page 86). Dip the bottom of each wonton crescent in flour. Place on a floured oven tray and cover with a damp dish towel.
For sauce, combine chili sauce and soy sauce.
Heat 1 tbsp oil in the wok over medium heat. When oil is very hot, add half the wonton crescents flat-side down to the wok in a single layer. Cook until crispy underneath, 5 minutes. Add enough water to the center of the wok to come about halfway up the sides of each wonton crescent. Cover wok with the lid and cook until all the liquid has evaporated, 10 minutes. Remove wontons from wok, cover with foil, and keep warm in a preheated 250°F oven. Repeat with remaining oil, wonton crescents, and water. Serve warm with chili soy dipping sauce.

THINK AHEAD
Assemble wonton crescents up to 3 hours in advance. Store covered with plastic on a floured oven tray in the refrigerator. Alternatively, freeze (see page 149) up to 1 month in advance. Defrost overnight in the refrigerator. Fry up to 45 minutes before serving. Keep warm, covered in a preheated 250°F oven.

COOKS' NOTE
It's the flour that makes the wonton crescents crispy. If assembling ahead of time, dip the wonton crescents again in flour before cooking for maximum crispiness.

CRISPY WONTON CRESCENT VARIATION

CRISPY WONTON CRESCENTS WITH HERBED SHRIMP AND TANGY LIME DIPPING SAUCE

For herbed shrimp filling, place 2½ oz cooked and peeled shrimp, 2 chopped scallions, 2 tbsp chopped cilantro, ½-inch piece ginger, grated, and 1 tbsp fish sauce in food processor or blender; pulse until finely chopped. Fill 1 recipe wonton wrappers or 20 store-bought dumpling wrappers as directed in the main recipe. Fry crescents as directed in the main recipe. For the tangy lime dipping sauce, combine juice of 1 lime with 1 tbsp sugar and 2 tbsp fish sauce. Serve wonton crescents warm with tangy lime dipping sauce.

TEXAS RED BEAN WRAPS WITH CILANTRO CREMA

MAKES 20

FOR BEAN FILLING

2 scallions

½ of a 15.5oz can of red kidney beans, drained

1 garlic clove, chopped

¼ tsp tabasco

juice of 1 lime

salt, black pepper

FOR CREMA

⅓ cup cream cheese

1 cup cilantro leaves, chopped

1 green chili, seeded and chopped

½ tbsp olive oil

4 - 8-inch flour tortillas

Roughly chop the white parts of the scallions. Reserve the green ends for the crema. For bean filling, place chopped scallion, beans, garlic, tabasco, and lime in a food processor or blender; pulse until well blended but still retaining some texture. Add salt and pepper to taste. Roughly chop the reserved green ends of the scallion. For crema, place chopped scallions, cream cheese, cilantro, chili, and oil in a food processor or blender; pulse until smooth. Heat a dry heavy-bottomed frying pan over medium heat. Place 1 tortilla in the pan. Cook until warm, 15 seconds. Flip tortilla over and warm other side, 15 seconds. Remove from pan and cover with a clean dish towel. Repeat with remaining tortillas.

Spread 1 warm tortilla first with 1 tbsp bean filling, then with 1 tbsp crema filling. Roll up tortilla gently, but firmly, as you would a jelly roll. Wrap securely in plastic wrap (see page 148). Twist the ends to secure. Repeat with remaining tortillas and filling. Refrigerate tortilla rolls 1 hour.

Trim messy ends with a serrated knife. Cut each tortilla wrap diagonally into 5 slices. Discard the plastic wrap after slicing. Serve chilled or at room temperature.

THINK AHEAD

Make wraps up to 1 day in advance. Refrigerate. Slice up to 1 hour before serving. Discard the plastic wrap just before serving to keep tortilla wraps moist.

COOKS' NOTE

One word of wrap advice: Do not overfill. If some filling does ooze out as you roll, simply scrape the excess off with the back of a knife.

ROAST PEPPER, GOAT CHEESE, AND MINT WRAPS

MAKES 20

1 red pepper, quartered and seeded

4 - 8-inch flour tortillas

⅓ cup fresh creamy goat cheese

¼ cup mint leaves, chopped

salt, black pepper

Grill and peel pepper quarters (see page 147). Cut peeled pepper quarters into julienne strips (see page 147).

Heat a dry heavy-bottomed frying pan over medium heat. Place 1 tortilla in the pan. Cook until warm, 15 seconds. Flip tortilla over and warm other side, 15 seconds. Remove from pan and cover with a clean tea towel. Repeat with remaining tortillas.

Spread 1 warm tortilla with 1 tbsp goat cheese. Top with a quarter of the pepper julienne strips. Sprinkle with mint and a pinch each salt and pepper. Roll up tortilla gently but firmly as you would a jelly roll. Wrap securely in plastic wrap (see page 148). Twist the ends to secure. Repeat with remaining tortillas and filling. Refrigerate tortilla rolls 1 hour.

Trim messy ends with a serrated knife. Cut each tortilla wrap diagonally into 5 slices. Discard the plastic wrap after slicing. Serve chilled or at room temperature.

THINK AHEAD

Make wraps up to 4 hours in advance. Refrigerate. Slice up to 1 hour before serving. Discard plastic wrap just before serving to keep tortilla wraps moist.

CREPES

MAKES 5

½ cup all-purpose flour
¼ tsp salt
1 egg, beaten
⅔ cup milk
2 tbsp butter

ESSENTIAL EQUIPMENT
9-inch nonstick frying pan

Sift flour and salt into a bowl. Make a well in the center and add the egg. Gradually beat in flour from the sides. Beating constantly, slowly pour in the milk to make a smooth batter. Cover and let stand at room temperature for 30 minutes.
Melt butter in the pan over medium heat. Swirl butter to coat bottom of pan. Pour excess melted butter into a bowl and reserve.
Pour a small ladle of batter into the pan. Tilt the pan and swirl the batter to cover the entire base of the pan. Cook until golden underneath, 1 minute. Flip crepe over with a rubber spatula and cook until golden underneath, 30 seconds more. Remove from pan. Repeat with reserved butter and remaining batter. Discard any thick or torn crepes.

THINK AHEAD
Make crepes up to 2 days in advance. Store in an airtight container stacked in single layers separated by waxed paper. Alternatively, freeze crepes up to 1 month in advance. Store in a sealed plastic freezer bag stacked in single layers separated by plastic wrap (see page 149). Defrost overnight in refrigerator.

COOKS' NOTE
Be sure to add the milk gradually while beating constantly in order to achieve a perfectly smooth batter. If lumps do occur, pour the batter through a strainer. Alternatively, make batter in a food processor or blender; pulse flour, salt, eggs, and milk until smooth.

ROLLED SMOKED HAM CREPES WITH TARRAGON AND MUSTARD CREAM

MAKES 20

½ cup cream cheese
1 tbsp grainy mustard
1 tbsp roughly chopped tarragon leaves
salt, black pepper
1 recipe crepes (see left)
5 slices smoked ham

Combine cream cheese, mustard, and tarragon. Add salt and pepper to taste. Spread crepes with cheese mixture. Roll up each ham slice tightly. Place 1 tightly rolled ham slice along the edge of 1 crepe. Roll crepe firmly around ham. Wrap in plastic wrap. Twist the ends to secure. Repeat with remaining filling, ham and crepes. Refrigerate rolls 1 hour. Trim messy ends with a serrated knife. Cut each rolled crepe into 4 slices, alternating between diagonal and straight cuts. Discard the plastic wrap after slicing. Serve chilled or at room temperature.

THINK AHEAD
Make rolled crepes up to 1 day in advance. Refrigerate. Cut up to 1 hour before serving.

ROLLED RICOTTA AND SAGE CREPES WITH PARMESAN SHAVINGS

MAKES 20

FOR CREPES
½ cup all-purpose flour
¼ tsp salt
1 egg, separated
1 cup milk
1 tbsp melted butter
1 tbsp finely chopped sage leaves

FOR FILLING
¾ cup ricotta cheese
1 tbsp finely chopped sage leaves
1 tbsp finely chopped parsley leaves
1 tbsp grated Parmesan cheese
salt, black pepper, nutmeg
4 tbsp butter
20 Parmesan shavings to garnish
  (see page 148)

For crepes, place flour, salt, egg yolk, milk, butter, and sage with a pinch of salt in a food processor or blender; pulse until smooth. Beat egg white until soft peaks form (see page 141). Fold a third of the batter into the beaten egg white until lightened. Fold in remaining batter until well combined. Cover and refrigerate for 30 minutes.
For filling, combine ricotta, herbs, and Parmesan until well combined. Add salt, pepper, and nutmeg to taste.
Melt butter in the pan over a medium heat. Swirl butter to coat bottom of pan. Pour excess melted butter into a bowl and reserve. Pour a small ladle of batter into the pan. Tilt the pan and swirl the batter to cover the entire bottom of the pan. Cook until golden underneath, 1 minute. Flip crepe over with a rubber spatula and cook until golden underneath, 30 seconds more. Remove from pan. Repeat with reserved butter and remaining batter until used up. Discard any thick or torn crepes. Cool crepes completely. Spread ricotta mixture evenly over crepes. Roll up tightly (see page 148). Wrap in plastic wrap. Twist the ends to secure. Refrigerate rolls 1 hour. Trim messy ends with a serrated knife. Cut each rolled crepe into 4 slices. Discard the plastic wrap after slicing. Garnish with Parmesan shavings. Serve chilled or at room temperature.

THINK AHEAD
Roll crepes up to 1 day in advance. Cover and refrigerate. Cut and garnish up to 1 hour before serving.

CHIVE-TIED CREPE BUNDLES WITH SMOKED SALMON AND LEMON CREME FRAICHE

MAKES 20

20 long chives
1 recipe crepes (see page 93)
grated zest of 1 lemon
½ cup crème fraîche or sour cream
½ lb smoked salmon slices, chopped
2 tbsp finely chopped chives
black pepper

ESSENTIAL EQUIPMENT
3¼-inch plain pastry cutter

Drop long chives into a pan of boiling water. Drain and rinse immediately under cold water. Pat dry on paper towel. Cut out 4 rounds from each crepe with the pastry cutter. Combine lemon zest and crème fraîche or sour cream. Place 1 tsp crème fraîche and 1 tsp smoked salmon in the center of each crepe round. Sprinkle with chives and a pinch of black pepper. Carefully bring the edges of each crepe together into a little bundle. Tie each bundle with a long chive. Refrigerate until chilled, 15 minutes.

THINK AHEAD
Make crepe bundles up to 4 hours in advance. Store in single layers covered with plastic wrap in the refrigerator.

COOKS' NOTE
To make classic beggars' purses, omit chopped chives and pepper and substitute sour cream for crème fraîche and black caviar for salmon.

MINI PEKING DUCK PANCAKES WITH PLUM SAUCE

MAKES 20

1 tsp honey
1 tsp light soy sauce
1 duck breast, skinned
1½-inch piece fresh ginger
2 scallions
½ cucumber, halved and seeded
20 long chives
10 store-bought Chinese pancakes
2 tbsp plum sauce

Preheat oven to 400°F.
Combine honey and soy. Brush duck with honey soy mixture. Roast duck until browned but still pink and juicy inside, 10 minutes. Cool. Slice duck breast diagonally into ¼-inch thick slices.
Cut ginger, scallions, and cucumber into julienne strips (see page 147). Drop chives into a pan of boiling water. Drain immediately and cool in cold water. Drain and pat dry with paper towels.
Cut pancakes in half. Trim a ¼-inch strip from the round edge of each pancake half to make 20 straight-sided pieces. Spread ¼ tsp plum sauce in center of each piece. Divide duck slices and julienne strips among pancake strips. Roll up tightly and tie with a chive. Serve at room temperature.

THINK AHEAD
Roast duck breast up to 1 day in advance. Cover and refrigerate. Cut vegetables and blanch chives up to 1 day in advance. Store in an airtight container in the refrigerator. Slice duck and roll pancakes up to 1 hour in advance.

HERBED ARTICHOKE AND PARMESAN FILO ROLLS WITH LIGHT LEMON MAYONNAISE DIP

MAKES 20

1 cup artichoke hearts in oil, drained	2 garlic cloves, crushed
1¼ cups grated Parmesan cheese	¼ tsp salt
1 egg, beaten	¼ tsp black pepper
2 tbsp finely chopped parsley leaves	10 sheets filo pastry
2 tbsp finely chopped oregano leaves	3 tbsp butter, melted
	1 recipe light lemon mayonnaise (see page 142)

Preheat oven to 350°F.

For filling, place artichokes, cheese, egg, chopped herbs, garlic, salt, and pepper in food processor; pulse until blended. Brush butter on both sides of 3 filo sheets and stack them together. Cut stacked filo sheets into 6-inch widths. Spread 1½ tsp of filling in a thin strip along the short end of the stacked filo. Roll the filo 1½ times around the filling (see below right). Brush with butter to seal. Place the filo roll seamside down on a buttered baking sheet. Repeat the rolling process with the remaining filling and butter to make about 5 or 6 rolls per filo stack. Repeat buttering and layering with the remaining filo sheets, spreading and rolling with the remaining filling until you have run out of ingredients. Brush finished filo rolls with more butter. Bake until crisp and golden, 15 minutes. Cool on a wire rack. Serve at warm or at room temperature with light lemon mayonnaise for dipping.

THINK AHEAD
Assemble up to 1 day in advance.
Store covered in single layers not touching.
Alternatively, assemble rolls and freeze up to
1 month in advance (see page 149). Bake frozen,
20–25 minutes.

COOKS' NOTE
If allowed to dry out, filo pastry becomes brittle and difficult to handle, so be sure to cover with a damp dish towel until ready to use.

MINTED FETA AND PINE NUT FILO ROLLS WITH LEMON AIOLI

MAKES 20

¾ cup pine nuts	1 tbsp lemon juice
¾ cup crumbled feta cheese	¼ tsp black pepper
2 tbsp grated Parmesan cheese	2 tbsp butter, melted
2 tbsp finely chopped mint leaves	5 sheets filo pastry
grated zest of ½ lemon	1 recipe lemon aioli (see page 142)

Preheat oven to 350°F.

For filling, toast pine nuts in a dry pan over a low heat until nutty and golden, 5 minutes. Cool. Place pine nuts, feta, Parmesan, mint, lemon zest and juice, and pepper in a food processor; pulse until well blended.

Brush butter on both sides of 3 filo sheets and stack them together. Cut stacked filo sheets into 6-inch widths. Spread 2 tsp filling in a thin strip along the short end of the stacked filo. Roll the filo 1½ times around the filling. Brush with butter to seal. Cut the finished roll in half. Place the 2 filo rolls seam-side down on a buttered baking sheet. Repeat the rolling process with the remaining filling and butter to make about 10 or 12 rolls per filo stack. Repeat buttering and layering with the remaining filo sheets, spreading and rolling with the remaining filling until you have run out of ingredients.

Brush filo rolls with butter. Bake until crisp and golden, 15 minutes. Cool on a wire rack. Serve at warm or at room temperature, with lemon aioli for dipping.

THINK AHEAD
Assemble up to 1 day in advance. Store covered in single layers not touching and refrigerate. Alternatively, assemble rolls and freeze up to 1 month in advance (see page 149). Bake frozen, 20–25 minutes.

STACKS & CASES

FILO TARTLETS

MAKES 20
4 sheets filo pastry
2 tbsp melted butter
ESSENTIAL EQUIPMENT
pastry brush, 2 - 12-cup mini muffin pans

Preheat oven to 350°F. Brush two sheets of filo pastry with the melted butter and lay one on top of the other (see right, top). With a sharp knife cut into 2 x 2-inch squares (see right, center). Butter the muffin cups and line each one with 3 buttered filo pastry squares placed at slightly different angles (see right, bottom). Repeat until all the filo pastry has been used. Bake to a deep golden brown, 6–8 minutes. Carefully remove the tartlets from the cups and leave to cool completely on a wire rack.

THINK AHEAD
Bake tartlets up to 1 month in advance. Store in an airtight container at room temperature.

COOKS' NOTE
To prevent the filo pastry from drying out, cover with a damp dish cloth until ready to use. If the buttered filo sticks to your fingers, use the pastry brush to press the filo squares into the muffin cups.

FILO TARTLETS WITH BANG BANG CHICKEN

MAKES 20
2 tbsp sesame seeds
4 tbsp smooth peanut butter
1 garlic clove, crushed
2-inch piece fresh ginger, chopped
2 tbsp lemon juice
1 tbsp dark soy sauce
¼ tsp tabasco
1 boneless, skinless chicken breast
1 recipe filo tartlets (see above)
1 scallion, finely sliced on the diagonal (see below, right)

Preheat oven to 350°F.
Toast seeds in a dry pan over low heat until nutty and golden, 3 minutes. Mix peanut butter, garlic, ginger, lemon juice, soy, and tabasco to a smooth sauce.
Put chicken in a pan with cold water to cover. Bring slowly to simmering point. Simmer gently without boiling until cooked through, 7–10 minutes. Cool completely in cooking liquid. Drain and cut chicken on the diagonal into ⅛-inch thick slices. Cut slices in half. Place 1 tsp bang bang sauce in each tartlet. Arrange chicken slices on top. Sprinkle with toasted seeds.
Garnish with scallion slices.

THINK AHEAD
Make sauce up to 3 days in advance. Cover and refrigerate. Cook chicken up to 1 day in advance. Cover and refrigerate. Fill tartlets up to 45 minutes before serving.

SLICING SCALLIONS
Trim scallion at both ends. Finely slice green stem at an angle to make sharp spikes.

FILO TARTLETS WITH SMOKED SALMON, CRACKED PEPPER, AND LIME

MAKES 20

⅓ lb smoked salmon slices
1 lime, peeled and segmented (see page 147)
½ cup crème fraîche or sour cream
1 recipe filo tartlets (see page 98)
juice of 1 lime
½ tsp cracked black peppercorns
½ cup chives, cut into ¾-inch strips, to garnish

Cut salmon slices into thin strips, ¼-inch wide. Cut lime segments into ½-inch pieces. Place 1 tsp crème fraîche in base of each tartlet. Top with smoked salmon strips. Sprinkle with a few drops of lime juice and cracked black pepper. Garnish with lime segments and chive strips.

THINK AHEAD
Fill tartlets up to 45 minutes before serving.

COOKS' NOTE
You can buy cracked black pepper, but it is easy to make yourself. Crush the peppercorns in a mortar with a pestle until cracked to tiny pieces rather than ground to a powder.

FILO TARTLETS WITH SMOKED CHICKEN, BLACK OLIVES, AND PARSLEY PESTO

MAKES 20

1 cup parsley leaves
1 clove garlic, crushed
4 tbsp pine nuts
4 tbsp grated Parmesan cheese
juice of ½ lemon
2 tbsp olive oil
salt, black pepper
1 smoked chicken breast
1 recipe filo tartlets (see page 98)
10 pitted black olives, halved

Place parsley, garlic, pine nuts, Parmesan, lemon juice, and oil in a food processor or blender; pulse to a thick paste. Add salt and pepper to taste. Cut chicken into thin strips, ¼-inch wide. Put 1 tsp pesto into each tartlet. Arrange chicken strips on top. Garnish with half an olive. Serve at room temperature.

THINK AHEAD
Make pesto up to 3 days in advance. Cover and refrigerate. Fill tartlets up to 45 minutes before serving.

FILO TARTLETS WITH CRAB, GINGER AND LIME

MAKES 20

1 tbsp sesame seeds
½ lb crab meat
1-inch piece fresh ginger, finely chopped
juice of 2 limes
1 cup cilantro leaves
¼ red pepper, cut into strips
4 tbsp mayonnaise (see page 142)
salt, tabasco
1 recipe filo tartlets (see page 98)
1 lime, peeled and segmented
  (see page 147)

Toast seeds in a dry pan over low heat until golden brown, 3 minutes. Toss crab with ginger, lime, cilantro, pepper, mayonnaise, and toasted seeds. Add salt and tabasco to taste. Cut lime segments into ½-inch pieces. Divide crab among filo tartlets. Garnish with lime segments. Serve at room temperature.

THINK AHEAD
Make filling up to 1 day in advance but only add cilantro up to 1 hour before serving.

FILO TARTLETS WITH SPICY CILANTRO SHRIMP

MAKES 20

2 tsp sesame seeds
¼ lb medium shrimp, cooked and peeled
¼ cup cilantro leaves, chopped
6 tbsp Thai sweet chili sauce
1 recipe filo tartlets (see page 98)

Toast seeds in a dry pan over low heat until golden brown, 3 minutes. Combine shrimp, cilantro, and chili sauce. Spoon into tartlets and garnish with toasted seeds.

THINK AHEAD
Make filling up to 1 day in advance. Cover and refrigerate. Fill tartlets up to 45 minutes before serving.

COOKS' NOTE
If using frozen cooked shrimp, defrost in a colander. When defrosted, squeeze out water with your hands and pat dry with paper towels.

FILO TARTLETS WITH ASIAN BEEF SALAD

MAKES 20

½ lb beef fillet steak, 1-inch thick
1 tbsp light soy sauce
1 tbsp lime juice
1 tbsp fish sauce
¼ tsp sugar
1 cup cilantro leaves
1 cup mint leaves
¼ red pepper, finely diced
1 tomato, seeded and diced (see page 147)
1 tsp sesame seeds
1 tsp grated lime zest
1 recipe filo tartlets (see page 98)
1 sliced red chili to garnish

Sear steak in hot pan on both sides, 6 minutes in total. Cool and cut into 20 slices. Toss steak slices with soy, lime zest, fish sauce, sugar, fresh herbs, pepper, tomato, seeds, and peel. Divide steak slices among filo tartlets. Garnish with red chili.

THINK AHEAD
Make filling up to 1 day in advance, but only add fresh herbs up to 1 hour before serving. Cover and refrigerate. Fill tartlets up to 45 minutes before serving.

CORN CUPS

MAKES 20
1 cup masa harina (see page 163)
½ tsp salt
⅔ cup warm water

ESSENTIAL EQUIPMENT
2½-inch plain pastry cutter;
2 - 12-cup mini muffin pans

Preheat oven to 400°F.
Place masa harina and salt in a bowl.
Pour in water and mix with a fork to
form a rough dough. Turn out onto
a clean surface and knead until
smooth and firm, 1 minute. Roll into
a smooth ball, cover with a dish
towel and let rest for 30 minutes.
Cut dough in half. Roll out 1 piece
of dough between 2 pieces of plastic
wrap to a ⅛-inch thickness. Peel off
the top layer of plastic wrap. Cut out
10 rounds with the pastry cutter.
Line 10 oiled mini-muffin cups with
the rounds. Repeat with remaining
dough and muffin cups. Bake until
crisp and dry, 20 minutes. Cool on a
wire rack.

THINK AHEAD
Bake cups up to 3 days in advance. Store in an
airtight container at room temperature.

COOKS' NOTE
Corn dough is an easy dough to work with. If the
dough should tear slightly as you line the muffin
cups, simply fill the hole with a scrap of dough.

CORN CUPS WITH PAPAYA, AVOCADO, AND PINK GRAPEFRUIT SALAD

MAKES 20
½ pink grapefruit, peeled and segmented
  (see page 147)
½ papaya, peeled
½ red onion, finely chopped
1 red chili, seeded and finely chopped
2 tbsp finely chopped mint leaves
1 tbsp red wine vinegar
2 tbsp sunflower oil
1 small avocado, peeled, pitted, and
  quartered
salt, black pepper
1 recipe corn cups (see left)

Cut each grapefruit segment into ½-inch
pieces. Cut papaya half into quarters.
Cut each papaya quarter into fine slices.
Combine grapefruit, papaya, onion, chili,
mint, vinegar, and oil. Cut each avocado
quarter into fine slices. Add to salad and
gently combine. Add salt and pepper to
taste. Divide among corn cups. Serve
chilled or at room temperature.

THINK AHEAD
Make salad up to 8 hours in advance, but add
mint no more than 3 hours in advance for best
color. Press plastic wrap directly onto the surface
of the salad and refrigerate. Fill corn cups just
before serving.

CORN CUPS WITH TUNA, MANGO, AND LIME CEVICHE

MAKES 20
6oz fresh tuna
juice of 2 limes
1 green chili, seeded and finely diced
½ medium red onion, finely chopped
1 mango, finely diced
2 tbsp finely chopped cilantro leaves
1 tsp salt
1 recipe corn cups (see far left)

Cut tuna into fine dice. Combine tuna
and lime in a nonmetallic bowl. Cover
and refrigerate, stirring occasionally, for
3 hours. Drain, discarding all but 1 tbsp
marinade. Combine tuna, chili, onion,
mango, cilantro, salt, and reserved
1 tbsp marinade. Divide among corn
cups. Serve chilled.

THINK AHEAD
Make ceviche up to 1 day in advance, but add
cilantro no more than 3 hours before serving for
best color. Cover and refrigerate. Fill corn cups just
before serving.

COOKS' NOTE
Fresh salmon, halibut, and scallops all make
excellent ceviche. If you are uncomfortable about
serving raw fish, use cooked, peeled shrimp instead.

CLAMS WITH GINGER AND LIME BUTTER

MAKES 20
6 tbsp butter, softened
½-inch piece fresh ginger,
 finely chopped
grated zest and juice of 1 lime
1 tbsp finely chopped cilantro leaves
salt, black pepper
20 clams
6 tbsp coarse salt

Combine butter, ginger, lime zest, and cilantro. Add salt and pepper to taste. Scrub clams under running water. Discard any that are broken or not tightly closed.
Place clams in a pan with 2 tbsp water and cover with lid. Steam over medium heat until open, 6 minutes. Shake pan occasionally to ensure even cooking. Remove clams with a slotted spoon. Discard any that are shut. Cool. Pry open with your fingers. Discard top shells. Loosen clams from bottom shells. Sprinkle a heatproof serving dish evenly with salt. Arrange half shells on salt. Divide butter among clams. Before serving, place clams under a preheated grill until butter melts, 2 minutes. Serve hot.

THINK AHEAD
Make butter up to 1 week in advance. Cover and refrigerate. Cook clams up to 1 day in advance. Cover and refrigerate. Top clams with butter up to 1 hour in advance. Grill and serve hot.

COOKS' NOTE
To barbecue clams, place unopened on a grill rack 6 inches above hot coals. When the shells open, the clams are done, 5 minutes. Discard top shell. Have the ginger and lime butter already melted and drizzle over the cooked clams. Cool slightly before serving or you might burn your fingers.

BACON-WRAPPED OYSTERS

MAKES 20
20 fresh oysters
½ lb bacon
1½ tbsp Worcestershire sauce
20 tbsp coarse salt

ESSENTIAL EQUIPMENT
20 wooden toothpicks

Preheat oven to 400°F.
Open the oysters (see below), reserving 20 bottom shells for serving.
Cut bacon slices across into 20 strips, each 1¾ inches long. Wrap a bacon strip around each oyster and secure with a toothpick. Place wrapped oysters on a baking sheet. Bake until bacon is lightly colored and cooked through, 10 minutes. Arrange oysters on reserved shells. To make a stable base for serving the oyster, place each half shell on 1 tbsp of coarse salt. Sprinkle oysters with Worcestershire sauce. Serve hot.

THINK AHEAD
Wrap oysters in bacon up to 2 hours in advance. Cover and refrigerate.

OPENING OYSTERS
Hold oyster flat side up in a dish towel. Insert a short, wide-bladed kitchen or oyster knife into the hinge of the oyster and twist to pry shell open. Scrape the oyster free from its top shell. Slice under flesh to detach the oyster from its bottom shell.

MUSSELS WITH SALSA CRUDA

MAKES 20
20 large fresh mussels
6 tbsp coarse sea salt
2 tomatoes, peeled, seeded, and diced
 (see page 147)
1 green chili, seeded and finely chopped
½ medium red onion, finely chopped
2 tbsp olive oil
1 tbsp lime juice
salt, black pepper
coarse sea salt for plating

Scrub mussels under running water. Discard any that are broken or not tightly closed. Pull off their beards with your fingers. Place mussels in a pan with 2 tbsp water and cover with lid. Steam over medium heat until open, 6 minutes. Shake pan occasionally to ensure even cooking. Remove mussels with a slotted spoon. Discard any that are shut. Cool. Pry open with your fingers. Discard top shells. Loosen mussels from bottom shells. Sprinkle serving dish evenly with coarse salt. Arrange mussels in half shells on salt. For salsa, combine tomatoes, chili, onion, lime, and oil. Add salt and pepper to taste. Spoon over mussels. Serve at room temperature or chilled.

THINK AHEAD
Cook mussels up to 1 day in advance. Cover and refrigerate. Make salsa up to 5 hours in advance. Cover and refrigerate. Top mussels up to 30 minutes before serving.

EGG AND BACON PUFFS

MAKES 35

½ lb bacon

1 hardboiled egg, halved

4 tbsp mayonnaise (see page 142)

⅓ cup chopped chives

salt, black pepper

1 recipe baked choux puffs
  (see pages 138–139)

Preheat oven to 350°F.
Place bacon on a foil-lined baking
sheet. Bake until golden and crisp,
about 10–15 minutes. Drain bacon on
paper towels, then cut into small dice.
Separate egg yolk from white. Cut
white into fine dice. Crush yolk with
fork. Combine bacon, white, mayonnaise,
and chives (reserving 2 tsp chives for
garnish). Add salt and pepper to taste.
Cut ¼-inch slice from the top of each
puff with a serrated knife. Spoon egg
and bacon mixture into puffs. Sprinkle
with egg yolk. Garnish with chives.
Serve at room temperature
or chilled.

THINK AHEAD
Make filling up to 1 day in advance. Cover
and refrigerate. Fill puffs up to 3 hours in
advance. Refrigerate. Garnish up to 45 minutes
before serving.

CLASSIC SHRIMP COCKTAIL PUFFS

MAKES 35

½ lb baby shrimp, cooked and peeled

3 tbsp mayonnaise (see page 142)

1 tbsp tomato ketchup

1 tsp Worcestershire sauce

salt, tabasco

1 recipe baked choux puffs
  (see pages 138-139)

2 small bibb lettuces or romaine hearts,
  separated into leaves

paprika for dusting

Combine shrimp, mayonnaise, ketchup,
and Worcestershire sauce. Add salt and
tabasco to taste. Cut ¼-inch slice from
top of each puff with a serrated knife.
Cut stalks from salad leaves and discard.
Cut each leaf into 1-inch pieces. Tuck
one lettuce piece into each puff. Spoon
shrimp mixture on top.
Dust with paprika. Serve at room
temperature or chilled.

THINK AHEAD
Make filling up to 1 day in advance. Cover
and refrigerate. Fill puffs up to 3 hours in
advance. Refrigerate. Garnish up to 45 minutes
before serving.

LIGHT LEMONY SALMON MOUSSE PUFFS

MAKES 35

½ lb salmon fillet

2 tbsp cream cheese

2 tsp horseradish sauce

2 tsp lemon juice

salt, white pepper

⅔ cup heavy cream

1 recipe baked choux puffs
  (see pages 138-139)

6 tbsp salmon caviar

35 dill sprigs to garnish

ESSENTIAL EQUIPMENT
piping bag with large star tip

Place salmon in pan of boiling water.
When water returns to a boil, remove
from heat immediately. Leave salmon in
water to cool completely. Drain on
paper towels. Place salmon with cream
cheese, horseradish, and lemon in a food
processor or blender; pulse until smooth.
Be careful not to over mix. Add salt and
pepper to taste. Whip cream until it holds
soft peaks (see page 144). Gently fold
salmon mixture into cream. Cut ¼-inch
slice from the top of each puff using a
serrated knife. Fill piping bag with mousse
(see page 146). Pipe mousse into puffs.
Garnish with salmon caviar and dill sprigs.
Serve chilled or at room temperature.

THINK AHEAD
Make filling up to 3 hours in advance. Cover and
refrigerate. Fill and garnish up to 1 hour in advance.

CARAMEL PROFITEROLES

MAKES 35

4 tbsp sugar
2 tbsp water
1 pint vanilla ice cream
1 recipe baked choux puffs (see pages 138–139)

ESSENTIAL EQUIPMENT
baking sheet lined with oiled baking parchment, melon baller

Put sugar and water in small pan and stir to dissolve. Bring to boil over medium heat. Cook to a light caramel (see page 145 and below, left). Dip each puff in caramel (see below, right). Place puffs dipped side down on the prepared baking sheet. Allow the caramel to set. Cut each dipped choux in half with a serrated knife.
With melon baller, scoop up 1 ball of ice cream. Sandwich the ice-cream ball between 2 halves of 1 choux puff. Repeat with remaining ice cream and puffs. Serve immediately.

THINK AHEAD
Dip puffs up to 3 hours in advance.

MINI ECLAIRS

MAKES 30

1 recipe baked choux mini éclairs (see pages 138–139)
1 recipe chocolate pastry cream (see page 145)
3½ oz semisweet chocolate

Pierce a small hole in underside of each éclair. Fill piping bag with pastry cream (see page 146). Pipe cream into pierced hole in each éclair (see below, left). Melt chocolate (see page 145). Remove from hot water. Hold base of each éclair between finger and thumb. Dip each éclair's upper surface into the chocolate. Remove quickly and allow excess chocolate to drip off (see below, right). Place on a wire rack, until chocolate is set. Serve cold or at room temperature.

THINK AHEAD
Fill and dip up to 1 day in advance. Cover and refrigerate. Alternatively, bake and freeze mini choux éclairs up to 3 weeks in advance. Crisp from frozen in a preheated 350°F oven for 3 minutes. Cool completely before filling and dipping.

COOK TO A LIGHT CARAMEL

DIP EACH PUFF IN CARAMEL

FILLING ECLAIRS

DIPPING ECLAIRS

CROUSTADES

MAKES 20
7 thin slices white bread
2 tbsp melted butter

ESSENTIAL EQUIPMENT
1 rolling pin, 1 - 2-inch fluted pastry cutter,
2 - 12-cup muffin pans

Preheat oven to 400°F. Roll out bread
slices thinly with the rolling pin. Cut
out 3 rounds from each slice using
the pastry cutter. Line each hole of
1 muffin tin with a bread round.
Brush each round with butter. Press
the empty muffin tin on top. Bake until
golden brown and crisp, 10 minutes.
Repeat with remaining bread.

THINK AHEAD
Make up to 3 days in advance. Store in an
airtight container at room temperature.

COOKS' NOTE
Put your pasta machine to unusual but most
efficacious use by rolling out the bread in it. Set
machine on the third setting and roll the bread slices
through twice. Cut out rounds according to the recipe.

MINI CAESAR SALAD CROUSTADES

MAKES 20
2 romaine hearts, leaves separated
2 tbsp mayonnaise (see page 142)
dash of Worcestershire sauce
squeeze of lemon juice
5 drained anchovy fillets, finely chopped
1 tbsp grated Parmesan cheese
1 recipe croustades (see left)
20 Parmesan shavings to garnish
  (see page 148)

Stack salad leaves and roll up tightly.
Slice across roll to make ¼-inch strips.
Flavor mayonnaise with Worcestershire
sauce and lemon juice. Toss salad with
mayonnaise, anchovies and grated
parmesan. Fill croustades with salad.
Garnish with Parmesan shavings.

THINK AHEAD
Prepare salad leaves up to 1 day in advance. Store
in an airtight container in the refrigerator. Fill
croustades up to 1 hour before serving.

TOMATO CONCASSEE WITH CREME FRAICHE AND CHIVES CROUSTADES

MAKES 20
3 ripe tomatoes, peeled, seeded and diced
  (see page 147)
2 tbsp finely chopped chives
2 tbsp crème fraîche or sour cream
2 tbsp lemon juice
tabasco
salt, black pepper
1 recipe croustades (see far left)

Combine tomatoes with chives, crème
fraîche or sour cream, lemon, and a dash
of tabasco. Cover and refrigerate for
1 hour. Add salt and pepper to taste.
Spoon concassée into croustades.
Serve cold.

THINK AHEAD
Make concassée the day before, but only add
salt and pepper just before using. Store in an
airtightcontainer in the refrigerator. Fill croustades
up to 45 minutes before serving.

POACHED SALMON WITH DILL MAYONNAISE CROUSTADES

MAKES 20

⅔ lb salmon fillet
1 recipe croustades (see page 108)
salt, white pepper
6 tbsp mayonnaise (see page 142)
2 tbsp finely chopped dill
20 dill sprigs to garnish

Place salmon in pan of boiling water. When water returns to boil, remove from heat at once and let cool completely. Drain salmon on paper towels. Separate into large flakes. Divide salmon among croustades. Sprinkle with salt and white pepper. Combine mayonnaise and dill. Spoon mayonnaise over salmon. Garnish with dill sprigs. Serve at room temperature.

THINK AHEAD
Cook salmon up to 3 days in advance. Cover and refrigerate. Fill croustades up to 45 minutes before serving.

COOKS' NOTE
Use very finely chopped cilantro and a squeeze of lime in place of dill to create a subtle Asian flavor.

QUAIL EGG, CAVIAR, AND CHERVIL CROUSTADES

MAKES 20

10 quail eggs
6 tbsp mayonnaise (see page 142)
1 recipe croustades (see page 108)
6 tbsp black lumpfish caviar
6 tbsp red lumpfish caviar
20 sprigs of chervil or parsley to garnish

Cook quail eggs in pan of boiling water for 5 minutes. Drain and refresh in cold water. Peel and cut in half. Spoon mayonnaise into croustades. Place half a quail egg cut side up on top of the mayonnaise. Top with ½ tsp each black and red caviar. Garnish with herb sprigs. Serve at room temperature.

THINK AHEAD
Cook and peel eggs up to 2 days in advance. Cover with water and refrigerate. Fill croustades up to 45 minutes before serving.

COOKS' NOTE
As an alternative filling, try quail eggs with lemon hollandaise (see page 143), crispy crumbled bacon, and snipped chives.

USING A ZESTER
Press down lightly, drag or pull the zester across the lemon rind.

CHICKEN TONNATO WITH LEMON AND CAPERS CROUSTADES

MAKES 20

1 boneless, skinless chicken breast
2 tbsp drained tuna
2 drained anchovy fillets
2 tbsp mayonnaise (see page 142)
1 tsp lemon juice
salt, black pepper
1 recipe croustades (see page 108)
20 drained capers
zest of ½ lemon to garnish (see below)

ESSENTIAL EQUIPMENT
zester

Put chicken in pan with cold water to cover. Bring slowly to a simmer over medium-low heat. Simmer gently without boiling until cooked through, 7–10 minutes. Cool completely in cooking liquid. Drain and cut chicken into fine dice. For tonnato sauce, place tuna, anchovies, mayonnaise, and lemon in a food processor; pulse until smooth. Add salt and pepper to taste. Divide chicken among croustades. Spoon over sauce. Garnish with capers and lemon zest. Serve at room temperature.

THINK AHEAD
Make tonnato sauce up to 3 days in advance. Cover and refrigerate. Cook chicken up to 1 day in advance. Cover and refrigerate. Fill croustades up to 45 minutes before serving.

CARROT, HONEY, AND GINGER SOUP CUPS

MAKES 20

2 tbsp butter

6 cups carrots, chopped

1 onion, chopped

1 garlic clove, chopped

4-inch piece fresh ginger, chopped

3 celery sticks, chopped

salt, black pepper

4¼ cups chicken stock

1 tbsp honey

4 tbsp heavy cream

1 tbsp chopped chives to garnish

ESSENTIAL EQUIPMENT

20 espresso or demitasse cups

Melt butter in a pan over low heat. Add carrots, onion, garlic, ginger, and celery with a pinch of salt. Continue cooking covered until very soft, 20 minutes. Add stock and increase heat to a boil. Reduce heat and simmer until carrots are cooked through, 15 minutes. Cool slightly, then place in a food processor or blender; pulse to a smooth purée. Place a fine-mesh strainer over the rinsed-out pan and push the purée through. Discard remainder left behind. Add 2 tbsp water to the purée at a time to adjust the soup's thickness to the consistency of light cream. Heat soup through over a medium heat. Add honey, cream, salt, and pepper to taste. Ladle into cups. Sprinkle with chives to garnish. Serve hot.

THINK AHEAD
Make up to 2 days in advance. Cover and refrigerate.

COOK'S NOTE
Remember that this soup will be sipped from a cup and not served with a spoon. Add water as specified by the recipe to achieve the proper consistency for this.

CHILLED SPICED CHICKPEA SOUP CUPS WITH AVOCADO SALSA

MAKES 20

FOR SOUP	FOR SALSA
14½ oz can of chickpeas, drained	1 medium avocado, peeled and pitted
14½ oz can of tomatoes	½ medium red onion, finely chopped
½ cup whole-milk yogurt	
2 garlic cloves, crushed	1 tbsp finely chopped mint leaves
1 tsp ground cumin	
1 tbsp lemon juice	1 tbsp lemon juice
2 tbsp olive oil	1 tbsp olive oil
salt, cayenne pepper	salt, black pepper
ESSENTIAL EQUIPMENT	6 tbsp whole-milk yogurt
20 espresso or demitasse cups	

For soup, place chickpeas, tomatoes, yogurt, garlic, cumin, lemon, and oil in a food processor or blender; pulse to a smooth purée. Transfer purée to a bowl. Gradually add up to ½ cup water to adjust the soup's thickness to a sipping consistency. Add salt and pepper to taste. Cover and refrigerate for 30 minutes to allow flavors to blend. For salsa, cut avocado into fine dice. Combine avocado, onion, mint, lime, and oil. Add salt and pepper to taste. Cover and refrigerate for 15 minutes to allow flavors to blend. Ladle soup into cups. Top with 1 tsp each salsa and sour cream. Serve chilled.

THINK AHEAD
Make soup up to 2 days in advance. Cover and refrigerate. Make salsa up to 8 hours in advance. Cover tightly with plastic wrap and refrigerate.

COOKS' NOTE
To help keep the salsa from discoloring when making it in advance, press a piece of plastic wrap directly on to the surface of the salsa. It's the oxygen in the air that turns peeled avocado brown, so the less air that comes into contact with the salsa, the longer it will stay looking fresh.

FOCACCINE POCKETS WITH BLUE CHEESE AND ARUGULA

MAKES 20

1 recipe unbaked bread dough
 (see page 140)
1 cup crumbled Gorgonzola cheese
1 cup arugula leaves
2 tomatoes, seeded and diced
 (see page 147)
salt, black pepper
1 tbsp olive oil

ESSENTIAL EQUIPMENT
2-inch plain pastry cutter

Preheat oven to 400°F.
Roll out dough to a ⅛-inch thickness.
Cut out 40 rounds with the pastry
cutter. Place 20 dough rounds onto
a floured baking sheet. Top each
focaccina with 1 tsp cheese, 2 arugula
leaves, and ½ tsp diced tomato. Sprinkle
with salt and pepper. Place remaining
dough rounds on top. Press edges down
to seal. Dimple focaccine with your
fingertips. Bake until crisp and golden,
15 minutes. Brush with olive oil and
serve warm.

THINK AHEAD
Bake focaccine up to 1 day in advance. Store in an
airtight container. Crisp for 10 minutes in preheated
400°F oven and serve warm. Freeze unbaked (see
page 149) for up to 1 month in advance. Bake
frozen in preheated 400°F oven for 20 minutes.

FOCACCINE POCKETS WITH WILD MUSHROOMS AND THYME

MAKES 20

1 tbsp olive oil
2 shallots, finely chopped
1¼ cups roughly chopped wild mushrooms
1 tsp finely chopped thyme leaves
salt, black pepper
1 recipe unbaked bread dough
 (see page 140)
1 tsp coarse salt
3 thyme sprigs, roughly chopped

ESSENTIAL EQUIPMENT
2-inch plain pastry cutter

Preheat oven to 400°F.
Heat oil in a frying pan. Add shallots
and mushrooms. Stir fry over high heat
until softened, 5 minutes. Add chopped
thyme, salt, and pepper to taste.
Cool completely.
Roll out dough to a ⅛-inch thickness.
Cut out 40 rounds with pastry cutter.
Place 20 dough rounds onto a floured
baking sheet. Spoon wild mushrooms
onto rounds. Top with remaining dough
rounds. Press edges down to seal.
Sprinkle with coarse salt. Bake until
crisp and golden, 15 minutes. Garnish
with thyme sprigs and serve warm.

THINK AHEAD
Bake focaccine up to 1 day in advance. Store in an
airtight container. Crisp for 10 minutes in preheated
400°F oven. Freeze unbaked (see page 149) for up
to 1 month in advance. Bake from frozen in
preheated 400°F oven for 20 minutes.

FOCACCINE POCKETS WITH RAISINS, FENNEL, AND GRAPES

MAKES 20

½ cup raisins
1 recipe unbaked bread dough
 (see page 140)
30 black or red grapes, halved
2 tbsp fennel seeds

ESSENTIAL EQUIPMENT
2-inch plain pastry cutter

Preheat oven to 400°F.
Pour boiling water to cover over raisins
and leave to soak until plump,
30 minutes. Drain and discard water.
Roll out dough to a ⅛-inch thickness.
Cut out 40 rounds with the pastry
cutter. Place 20 dough rounds on
floured baking sheet. Cover with raisins
and top with remaining dough rounds.
Press edges down to seal. Top each
focaccina with 3 grape halves and
sprinkle with fennel seeds. Bake until
crisp and golden, 15 minutes.
Serve warm.

THINK AHEAD
Bake focaccine up to 1 day in advance. Store in an
airtight container. Crisp for 10 minutes in preheated
400°F oven and serve warm. Freeze unbaked (see
page 149) for up to 1 month in advance. Bake
frozen in preheated 400°F oven for 20 minutes.

MINI DOUBLE CHOCOLATE MERINGUE KISSES

MAKES 20

3½ oz semisweet chocolate

½ cup heavy cream

1 tbsp sugar

1 recipe chocolate meringue kisses
  (see page 141)

2 tsp cocoa powder for dusting

Melt chocolate (see page 145); cool. Whip cream until it holds soft peaks. Beat in sugar (see page 144). Hold 1 meringue by its pointed end and dip its flat underside in chocolate; repeat with another meringue. Sandwich two prepared meringues together with 1 tsp cream in between. Repeat with remaining meringues. Dust with cocoa powder. Serve at room temperature.

THINK AHEAD
Fill kisses up 2 hours in advance. Keep at room temperature until ready to serve.

MINI RASPBERRY RIPPLE MERINGUE KISSES

MAKES 20

½ cup heavy cream

1 tbsp sugar

1 cup raspberries

1 recipe vanilla meringue kisses
  (see page 141)

Whip cream until it holds soft peaks. Beat in sugar (see page 144). Crush raspberries with fork and gently fold into cream until cream is "rippled" with raspberry color. Hold 1 meringue by its pointed end and scoop up a little of the raspberry cream on its flat underside; repeat with another meringue. Sandwich two prepared meringues together. Repeat with remaining meringues. Refrigerate for 30 minutes to set cream. Serve chilled.

THINK AHEAD
Fill kisses up to 3 hours in advance. Cover and refrigerate.

MINI LEMON MERINGUE KISSES

MAKES 20

½ cup heavy cream

1 tbsp sugar

4 tbsp lemon curd

1 recipe vanilla meringue kisses
  (see page 141)

2 tsp powdered sugar to dust

Whip cream until it holds soft peaks. Beat in sugar (see page 144). Fold lemon curd into whipped cream. Hold 1 meringue by its pointed end and scoop up a little of the lemon cream on its flat underside; repeat with another meringue. Sandwich two prepared meringues together. Repeat with remaining meringues. Refrigerate for 30 minutes to set cream. Dust with powdered sugar to garnish. Serve chilled.

THINK AHEAD
Fill kisses up to 3 hours in advance. Cover and refrigerate. Dust with sugar just before serving.

MINI BURGER BUNS

MAKES 25

1 recipe unbaked bread dough
(see page 140)
1 egg yolk beaten with 1 tbsp water
1 tbsp sesame seeds

Preheat oven to 400°F. Divide dough into small walnut-sized pieces and shape into smooth rolls. Place on a floured baking sheet and press down gently to flatten to buns. Cover with a cloth and leave for 20 minutes until doubled in size. Brush each bun with beaten egg and sprinkle with sesame seeds. Bake until golden brown, 10 minutes. Cool on a wire rack.

THINK AHEAD
Bake buns up to 3 days in advance. Store in an airtight container at room temperature. Alternatively, shape and freeze buns. Bake frozen buns in preheated 400°F oven for 20 minutes.

COOKS' NOTE
No time for bread making? Buy full-size burger buns and cut in half. Cut out rounds from each half using a 1½-inch pastry cutter.

MINI HAMBURGERS WITH PICKLES AND KETCHUP

MAKES 25

10oz ground beef
1 tbsp very finely chopped onion
2 tbsp Worcestershire sauce
1 tsp Dijon mustard
1 tsp salt, ¼ tsp black pepper
4 tbsp tomato ketchup
1 recipe mini burger buns, halved
(see left)
2 romaine hearts, separated into leaves
10 cornichons, to garnish

Preheat oven to 400°F. Mix beef, onion, Worcestershire sauce, mustard, salt, and pepper and 1 tbsp ketchup until well combined. Divide mixture into 25 walnut-sized pieces. With wet hands, shape pieces into balls and flatten into burgers. Place on baking sheet and cook until browned and firm to the touch, 10 minutes. Cut stalks from lettuce leaves and discard. Cut leaves into 1-inch pieces. Cut cornichons on diagonal into thin slices. Place burgers on bottom halves of burger buns. Top with lettuce, cornichon slices, and ketchup. Gently press on top half of burger bun. Serve warm or at room temperature.

THINK AHEAD
Cut buns up to 1 day in advance. Store in an airtight container at room temperature. Shape burgers up to 1 day in advance. Cover and refrigerate. Assemble burgers up to 3 hours in advance.

COOKS' NOTE
When shaping the burgers, make sure to flatten them properly. If the mini burgers have a slightly domed top, the burger buns tend to topple off.

MINI TUNA BURGERS WITH WASABI MAYONNAISE AND PICKLED GINGER

MAKES 25

½ lb tuna steak, ½ inch thick
4 tbsp mayonnaise (see page 142)
1 tsp wasabi paste
¼ tsp soy sauce
¼ tsp rice vinegar
pinch sugar
25 pieces pickled ginger
25 cilantro leaves to garnish
1 recipe mini burger buns, halved
and toasted (see far left)

ESSENTIAL EQUIPMENT
cast-iron grill pan.

Cut tuna into 1-inch cubes. Preheat pan over a high heat. Sear tuna cubes on both sides until firm to touch, 2 minutes per side. Add salt and pepper to taste. Cool. Combine mayonnaise, wasabi, soy sauce, vinegar, and sugar. Divide mayonnaise mixture among bottom bun halves. Top with tuna pieces and garnish with ginger and cilantro leaves. Cover with top bun halves. Serve warm or at room temperature.

THINK AHEAD
Cut buns up to 1 day in advance. Store in an airtight container at room temperature. Assemble tuna burgers up to 2 hours in advance.

COOKS' NOTE
Grill the tuna for the best flavor. Place tuna on an oiled rack 3 inches above medium hot coals for 2 minutes on each side.

BASIC BOUCHEE RECIPE

MAKES 30

8oz puff pastry
1 egg yolk beaten with 1 tbsp water

ESSENTIAL EQUIPMENT
1¾-inch fluted pastry cutter,
1-inch fluted pastry cutter

Preheat oven to 400°F.
Roll out pastry to a ⅛-inch thickness.
Cut out 60 rounds with the larger
pastry cutter. With the smaller pastry
cutter, cut out a circle from the
center of half of the pastry rounds
(see below, left). This results in
30 pastry rounds and 30 pastry rings.
Brush the pastry rounds with the
beaten egg. Place pastry rings on
pastry rounds (see below, right).
Gently press to seal.
Place topped rounds on a floured
baking sheet. Brush again with egg.
Bake until risen and golden brown,
12 minutes. Cool on a wire rack. Cool
to room temperature before filling.

THINK AHEAD
Bake up to 1 week in advance. Store in an airtight
container in a single layer at room temperature.

TARRAGON AND MUSTARD LOBSTER BOUCHEES

MAKES 30

¼ lb cooked lobster meat, shredded
1 tomato, peeled, seeded and diced
 (see page 147)
2 tbsp chopped tarragon leaves
1 tsp Dijon mustard
4 tbsp mayonnaise (see page 142)
salt, black pepper
1 recipe baked bouchées (see left)

Combine lobster, tomato, tarragon,
mustard, and mayonnaise. Add salt and
pepper to taste. Use a teaspoon to fill
bouchées with lobster mixture. Serve at
room temperature.

THINK AHEAD
Make filling up to 1 day in advance. Cover and
refrigerate. Fill bouchées up to 30 minutes
before serving.

COOKS' NOTE
Chopped shrimp or crab meat are both
delicious substitutes for the lobster in this recipe.

WILD MUSHROOM, GARLIC, AND THYME BOUCHÉES

MAKES 30

1 tbsp butter
1½ cups finely chopped wild mushrooms
1 shallot, finely chopped
1 garlic clove, finely chopped
1 tsp finely chopped thyme leaves
2 tbsp crème fraîche or sour cream
salt, black pepper
1 recipe baked bouchées (see far left)
30 thyme sprigs to garnish

Melt butter in a frying pan over high
heat. Add mushrooms, shallots, garlic,
and thyme. Stir fry until tender and
slightly crisp, 5–10 minutes. Stir in
crème fraîche or sour cream and remove
from heat. Add salt and pepper to taste.
Use a teaspoon to fill bouchées with
mushroom mixture. Garnish with thyme.
Serve hot or at room temperature.

THINK AHEAD
Make filling up to 1 day in advance. Cover and
refrigerate. Warm through gently over a low heat with
1 tbsp extra crème fraîche. Fill bouchées up to
45 minutes in advance. Garnish just before serving.

WONTON CUPS

MAKES 20

1¼ cups all-purpose flour
½ cup boiling water

ESSENTIAL EQUIPMENT
2 - 12-cup mini muffin pans

Place the flour in a bowl and make a well in the center. Pour in the water and mix with a fork to form a rough dough. Cover with a dish towel and let stand until cool enough to handle. Knead on a lightly floured surface until smooth and elastic, 5 minutes. Cover with a dish towel and let rest for 30 minutes.
Preheat oven to 400°F.
Roll out dough on a lightly floured surface to a paper thin thickness. With a sharp knife, cut into about 20 squares, 2 x 2 inches each. Oil the muffin cups of both pans and line each one with a wonton pastry square. Bake until crisp, 10 minutes. Cool before removing from tins.

THINK AHEAD
Make up to 2 weeks in advance. Store in an airtight container at room temperature.

SQUID, SESAME, AND LIME WONTON CUPS

MAKES 20

2 tsp sesame seeds
1 tbsp sesame oil
1 tbsp sunflower oil
grated zest of ½ lime
juice of 1 lime
1 tsp fish sauce
1 scallion, finely chopped
⅓ lb baby squid rings
1 recipe wonton cups (see left)

Toast seeds in a dry pan over low heat until nutty and golden, 3 minutes. Cool. Combine toasted seeds, oils, lime zest and juice, fish sauce, and scallion; set aside. Bring a pan of water to a boil. Add the squid. When the water has returned to a boil, continue cooking for just 30 seconds. Drain and rinse under cold water. Dry on paper towels. Add squid to sesame lime dressing and stir to coat each ring well. Divide among wonton cups. Serve chilled or at room temperature.

THINK AHEAD
Make squid, sesame, and lime salad up to 1 day in advance. Cover and refrigerate. Fill wonton cups up to 1 hour before serving.

FIVE-SPICE DUCK AND PAPAYA WONTON CUPS

MAKES 20

1 tsp honey
½ tsp five-spice powder
1 tsp dark soy sauce
1 duck breast, skinned
1 tsp rice wine vinegar
1 tsp sesame oil
1 tsp soy sauce
1 recipe wonton cups (see far left)
½ papaya, peeled and diced
20 cilantro leaves to garnish

Preheat oven to 400°F. Combine honey, spice powder, and soy. Brush duck on both sides with honey-soy mixture. Roast for 10 minutes. Cool completely. Cut crosswise into very fine slices. Combine duck with vinegar, oil, and soy sauce. Stir to coat each slice well. Divide duck among wonton cups. Top with papaya dice and garnish with cilantro leaves.

THINK AHEAD
Cook and dress duck up to 1 day in advance. Cover and refrigerate. Dice papaya up to 1 day in advance. Cover and refrigerate. Fill wonton cups up to 1 hour in advance.

CUCUMBER CUPS WITH BLUE-CHEESE MOUSSE AND CRISPY BACON

MAKES 20

6 slices bacon

1 cups crumbled Roquefort cheese

½ cup cream cheese

salt, black pepper

1 scallion, cut into strips

1 recipe cucumber cups (see right)

ESSENTIAL EQUIPMENT
piping bag with large star tip

Preheat oven to 350°F.
Place bacon on foil-lined baking pan.
Cook until golden and crisp, about
10–15 minutes. Drain on paper towels
and cut into small triangular pieces.
Beat cheeses until smoothly blended.
Add salt and pepper to taste.
Fill piping bag with mousse (see
page 146) and pipe into cucumber cups.
Top with crispy bacon pieces. Garnish
with scallion strips.

THINK AHEAD
Prepare mousse up to 3 days in advance. Cover
and refrigerate. Cook bacon up to 1 day in advance.
Store in an airtight container in the refrigerator. Crisp
in a preheated 350°F oven for 2 minutes.
Fill cups up to 1 hour before serving.

CUCUMBER CUPS

MAKES 20

1 cucumber

ESSENTIAL EQUIPMENT
1½-inch fluted pastry cutter, melon baller
Cut cucumber into about 20 - ¾-inch-
thick slices. Cut each slice with the
pastry cutter (see opposite, left). Using
melon baller, scoop out soft centers to
make cups, leaving a ¼-inch layer as
a base (see opposite, right).

THINK AHEAD
Make cups up to 2 days in advance. Store in an airtight container in the refrigerator.

CUCUMBER CUPS WITH SMOKED TROUT MOUSSE, LEMON, AND DILL

MAKES 20

⅓ lb smoked trout

½ cup cream cheese

½ tsp grated lemon zest

1 tbsp lemon juice

cayenne pepper

1 recipe cucumber cups (see top of page)

1 tsp paprika for dusting

20 dill sprigs to garnish

ESSENTIAL EQUIPMENT
piping bag with large star tip

Place smoked trout, cream cheese, zest,
and juice in a food processor or blender;
pulse to a smooth paste. Add cayenne
pepper to taste. Fill piping bag with
mousse (see page 146) and pipe into
cucumber cups. Dust with paprika and
garnish with dill sprigs.

THINK AHEAD
Make mousse up to 1 day in advance. Cover and
refrigerate. Fill cups up to 1 hour before serving.

CUCUMBER BARQUETTES WITH SMOKED SALMON AND PICKLED GINGER

MAKES 20

¼ lb smoked salmon slices

20 pieces of pickled ginger

1 tsp wasabi

20 cucumber barquettes (see below)

Cut salmon into 20 - ¼-inch wide strips.
Put a piece of ginger on top of each
salmon strip and roll up. Put a dab of
wasabi on each cucumber boat. Top
with a smoked salmon roll.

THINK AHEAD
Fill barquettes up to 1 hour before serving.

MAKING BARQUETTES
Peel and cut cucumber
in half. Cut each half into
2-inch-length pieces.
Use tip of knife to trim
off ½ inch of flesh from
the inside of each piece.
Cut each piece into a
diamond shape, about
2 inches across.

CELERY BARQUETTES WITH STILTON AND WALNUTS

MAKES 20
8 large celery stalks
1 cup crumbled Stilton cheese
½ cup cream cheese
salt, black pepper
1 tsp paprika to dust
20 walnut pieces to garnish

ESSENTIAL EQUIPMENT
piping bag with large star tip

Cut celery stalks on diagonal to make 20 - 2 x 2-inch- diamond-shaped pieces. Beat Stilton and cream cheese until well combined. Add salt and pepper to taste. Fill piping bag with cheese mixture (see page 146) and pipe into celery barquettes. Dust with paprika and garnish with walnuts.

THINK AHEAD
Make filling up to 2 days in advance. Cover and refrigerate. Prepare barquettes up to 2 days in advance. Store in an airtight container in the refrigerator. Fill barquettes up to 1 hour before serving.

CHERRY TOMATOES WITH CRAB AND TARRAGON MAYONNAISE

MAKES 20
20 cherry tomatoes
½ lb crab meat
4 tbsp mayonnaise (see page 142)
1 tsp Dijon mustard
1 tbsp tarragon leaves, chopped
salt, black pepper

Cut and discard thin slices from stem end of tomatoes to make flat, stable bases. Cut and reserve thin slices from smooth end to make tomato lids. Scoop out seeds with teaspoon and discard. Turn tomatoes upside down on paper towels to drain for 5 minutes. Combine crab, mayonnaise, mustard, and tarragon. Add salt and pepper to taste. Use a teaspoon to fill tomatoes with crab mixture. Top with tomato lids.

THINK AHEAD
Prepare tomatoes up to 2 days in advance. Store in an airtight container in the refrigerator. Fill tomatoes up to 3 hours before serving. Cover and refrigerate.

RADISH CUPS WITH BLACK OLIVE TAPENADE

MAKES 20
1¼ cups pitted black olives
4 anchovy fillets
2 tbsp capers
1 garlic clove, finely chopped
1 tsp lemon juice
1 tsp finely chopped thyme leaves
2 tbsp olive oil
¼ tsp black pepper
20 round radishes

ESSENTIAL EQUIPMENT
melon ball cutter

Place olives, anchovies, capers, garlic, lemon juice, thyme, and oil in a food processor or blender; pulse to a thick paste. Add pepper. Cut and discard thin slices from radish bottoms to make flat, stable bases. Cut and reserve thin slices from radish tops to make radish lids. Using melon ball cutter, remove most of radish center to make "cups." Fill cups with tapenade. Top with reserved radish lids.

THINK AHEAD
Make filling up to 1 month in advance. Cover and refrigerate. Prepare cups up to 2 days in advance. Store in an airtight container in the refrigerator. Fill cups up to 1 hour before serving.

COOKS' NOTE
If you don't have radishes with tops, a sprig of dill will make a decorative and flavorful alternative garnish.

QUESADILLA TRIANGLES WITH SMOKY SHREDDED CHICKEN

MAKES 24

1 boneless, skinless chicken breast	1 tsp tomato purée
3 tbsp sunflower oil	½ tsp sugar
½ medium onion, finely chopped	salt, black pepper
2 garlic cloves, crushed	6 - 6-inch flour tortillas
½ tsp ground cumin	6 tbsp grated Gruyère cheese
½ tsp ground coriander	2 scallions, finely chopped
1 canned chipotle pepper in adobo sauce (see page 162), chopped	⅓ cup sour cream
7oz can of chopped tomatoes	24 cilantro leaves to garnish

ESSENTIAL EQUIPMENT
cast-iron grill pan

Place chicken in a pan with cold water to cover. Bring to a simmer over low heat. Simmer gently without boiling until cooked through, 7–10 minutes. Cool completely before draining. Drain and shred chicken.

Heat 2 tbsp oil in a skillet over medium heat. Stir fry onion until softened, 5 minutes. Add garlic, cumin, coriander, chipotle, tomato, tomato purée, and sugar. Cook until thickened, 5 minutes. Cool. Combine with shredded chicken. Add salt and pepper to taste.

Preheat grill pan over medium heat. Brush 1 side of a tortilla with oil. Place oiled side down onto the pan, pressing lightly with a spatula. Cook until just marked, 1 minute. Repeat with remaining tortillas.

Preheat oven to 400°F. Place half the tortillas on a baking sheet marked side down. Combine cheese and scallions. Sprinkle 1 tbsp cheese-onion mix, then 1 tbsp chicken over each tortilla. Sprinkle 1 tbsp cheese-onion mix over each topped tortilla. Top with remaining tortillas. Bake until cheese melts, 5 minutes. Cool slightly. Cut into 8 wedges with kitchen scissors or a serrated knife. Garnish triangles with sour cream and cilantro leaves. Serve warm or at room temperature.

THINK AHEAD
Make chicken up to 1 day in advance. Cover and refrigerate. Prepare tortillas and fill up to 1 hour before serving. Cover and keep at room temperature.

QUESADILLA TRIANGLES WITH HOT PEPPER RELISH

MAKES 24

6 - 6-inch flour tortillas	2 tbsp finely chopped cilantro leaves
1 tbsp sunflower oil	¼ tsp sugar
1 red pepper, quartered and seeded	salt, black pepper
2 green chilies, seeded and finely diced	6 tbsp grated Gruyère cheese
½ garlic clove, crushed	⅓ cup sour cream
1 tbsp olive oil	1 scallion to garnish
1 tbsp red wine vinegar	

ESSENTIAL EQUIPMENT
cast-iron grill pan

Preheat grill pan over medium heat. Brush 1 side of a tortilla with oil. Place tortilla oiled side down onto the pan, pressing lightly with a spatula. Cook until just marked, 1 minute. Repeat with remaining tortillas.

For relish, broil and peel pepper quarters (see page 147). Finely chop broiled pepper. Combine pepper with chili, garlic, oil, vinegar, cilantro, and sugar. Add salt and pepper to taste. Cover and let stand for 1 hour at room temperature to allow the flavors to blend. Preheat oven to 400°F.

Place half the tortillas on a baking sheet. Sprinkle with 1 tbsp cheese, then spread 1 tbsp relish over each tortilla. Sprinkle with another 1 tbsp cheese. Top with remaining tortilla. Bake until cheese melts, 5 minutes. Cool slightly.

For garnish, cut scallion diagonally into ½-inch pieces. Cut each quesadilla into 8 wedges with kitchen scissors or a serrated knife. To garnish, top quesadilla triangles with sour cream and a piece of scallion. Serve warm or at room temperature.

THINK AHEAD
Make salsa up to 1 day in advance. Cover and refrigerate. Prepare tortillas and fill up to 1 hour before serving. Cover and keep at room temperature.

COOKS' NOTE
We recommend wearing rubber gloves when working with chilies. Capsaicin, the substance in chilies that makes them hot and spicy, can cause a painful burning sensation if brought into contact with eyes or sensitive skin.

MINI MUFFINS

MAKES 20

1½ cups all-purpose flour
1 tsp baking powder
1 tsp baking soda
¼ tsp salt
6 tbsp sugar
1 egg, beaten
½ cup milk
3 tbsp melted butter

ESSENTIAL EQUIPMENT
2 - 12-cup mini muffin pans, buttered

Preheat oven to 400°F.
Sift flour, baking powder, baking soda, and salt into a bowl. Make a well in the center. Add remaining ingredients, plus additional flavoring, if using. Gently fold everything together to make a wet batter. Spoon batter into 20 of the buttered muffin cups. Bake until golden brown and firm to the touch, 12 minutes. Turn out and cool completely on a wire rack.

THINK AHEAD
Bake muffins up to 1 day in advance. Store in an airtight container.

COOKS' NOTES
When flavored, we think these mini muffins are delicious enough to be served without a filling. Place in a preheated 350°F oven for 5 minutes before serving.

FLAVORED MUFFIN VARIATIONS

ORANGE MUFFINS
Add grated zest of 1 orange to ingredients.

ROSEMARY MUFFINS
Add 2 tsp finely chopped rosemary leaves to ingredients.

ORANGE MUFFINS WITH SMOKED TURKEY AND CRANBERRY SAUCE

MAKES 20

1 recipe orange mini muffins (see left)
½ cup cream cheese
⅛ lb smoked turkey slices
4 tbsp cranberry sauce

Cut muffins in half. Spread each bottom half with cream cheese. Cut turkey slices into 20 - 1-inch-wide strips. Place 1 turkey strip onto each muffin. Spoon sauce on top. Cover with top half of muffin. Serve at room temperature.

THINK AHEAD
Fill muffins up to 3 hours before serving. Store at room temperature.

ROSEMARY MINI MUFFINS WITH SMOKED HAM AND PEACH RELISH

MAKES 20

1 recipe rosemary mini muffins (see far left)
1 peach, fresh or canned
1 tsp cider vinegar
4 tbsp cream cheese
⅛ lb smoked ham slices

For relish, cut peach into fine dice. Toss with vinegar. Cut muffins in half. Spread each bottom half with cream cheese. Cut ham slices into 20 - 1-inch-wide strips. Place 1 ham strip onto each muffin. Spoon peach relish on top. Cover with top half of muffin. Serve at room temperature.

THINK AHEAD
Fill muffins up to 3 hours before serving. Store at room temperature.

COOKS' NOTE
We highly recommend the combination of smoked duck and red-currant jelly as an alternative filling for these flavorful rosemary mini muffins.

BABY BAGELS

MAKES 20
1 recipe unbaked bread dough
  (see page 140)
1 egg yolk beaten with 1 tbsp water
2 tbsp poppy or sesame seeds

ESSENTIAL EQUIPMENT
Slotted spoon

Preheat oven to 400°F.
Divide dough into 20 walnut-sized pieces. Shape each piece into a ball. Form each ball into a ring by inserting a floured finger into the center (see below). Work your finger in a circle to stretch and widen the hole. Bring a pan of water to a boil over high heat, then reduce heat to simmering. Working in batches, use the slotted spoon to lower bagels into the water. Boil until bagels rise to surface, about 1 minute. Remove from water to an oiled baking sheet with the slotted spoon. Repeat with remaining bagels. Brush bagels with beaten egg and sprinkle with seeds. Bake until golden, 10 minutes.

THINK AHEAD
Bake bagels up to 3 days in advance. Store in an airtight container. Freeze bagels up to 1 month in advance.

FORM EACH BALL INTO A RING
Insert floured finger into the center. Work finger in a circle to widen the hole.

BABY BAGELS WITH CREAM CHEESE, LOX, AND DILL

MAKES 20
1 recipe baby bagels (see left)
½ cup cream cheese
½ lb smoked salmon
20 dill sprigs
black pepper

Slice bagels in half and toast lightly. Spread bottom halves with cream cheese. Top with salmon and dill and sprinkle with pepper. Cover with top halves. Serve at room temperature.

THINK AHEAD
Fill bagels up to 5 hours in advance. Cover and store at room temperature.

BABY BAGELS WITH ROASTED RED ONION, GOAT CHEESE, AND CHIVES

MAKES 20
2 red onions, roughly chopped
1 tbsp olive oil
salt, black pepper
1 recipe baby bagels (see far left)
½ cup fresh creamy goat cheese
½ cup chives, roughly chopped

Preheat oven to 400°F.
Toss onions with oil, salt, and pepper. Roast onions until soft, 15 minutes. Slice bagels in half and toast lightly. Spread each bottom half with goat cheese. Sprinkle with salt and pepper. Top with red onions and chives. Cover with top halves. Serve at room temperature.

THINK AHEAD
Fill bagels up to 5 hours in advance. Cover and store at room temperature.

CHOCOLATE CUPS WITH KIWI, RASPBERRY, AND LIME MOUSSE

MAKES 20
½ cup cream cheese
juice and grated zest of 2 limes
¼ cup sugar
½ cup heavy cream
20 store-bought mini chocolate cups
½ kiwi fruit, peeled, to garnish
10 raspberries, halved, to garnish

ESSENTIAL EQUIPMENT
piping bag with large star tip

Beat cream cheese with juice, zest, and sugar until smooth. Whip cream until it holds soft peaks (see page 144). Fold cream into cream cheese mixture. Fill piping bag with mousse and pipe into chocolate cups (see page 146).
Cut kiwi crosswise into ¼-inch slices. Cut each slice into eighths. Garnish with kiwi triangles and raspberry halves.

THINK AHEAD
Fill cups up to 1 day in advance. Cover and refrigerate. Garnish up to 1 hour before serving.

CHOCOLATE CUPS WITH WHITE CHOCOLATE MOUSSE

MAKES 20
½ cup heavy cream
1 egg white
4oz white chocolate, melted (see page 145)
20 store-bought mini chocolate cups
2 tbsp white chocolate flakes
1 tsp cocoa powder for dusting

Whip cream until it holds soft peaks (see page 144). Beat egg white until it holds soft peaks. Fold melted chocolate into beaten whites, then fold in the whipped cream. Spoon mousse into chocolate cups. Refrigerate until set, about 1 hour. Garnish with white chocolate flakes and a dusting of cocoa.

THINK AHEAD
Fill cups up to 1 day in advance. Cover and refrigerate. Garnish up to 1 hour before serving.

COOKS' NOTE
To make chocolate flakes, grate white chocolate over the fine-grate side of a cheese grater. To prevent the chocolate flakes from melting in your fingers, refrigerate the piece of chocolate briefly before you begin and hold the chocolate with a piece of waxed paper as you grate. Use a teaspoon to sprinkle the flakes over each chocolate cup.

CHOCOLATE CUPS WITH MANGO AND MASCARPONE CREAM

MAKES 20
1 mango, peeled and sliced (see page 163)
½ cup mascarpone cheese
juice of ½ lime
1 tbsp sugar
20 store-bought mini chocolate cups
20 tiny mint sprigs to garnish

ESSENTIAL EQUIPMENT
piping bag with large star tip

Place mangoes, mascarpone, lime, and sugar in a food processor or blender; pulse to a smooth purée. Fill piping bag with mango and mascarpone cream (see page 146). Pipe into chocolate cups. Garnish with mint sprigs.

THINK AHEAD
Fill cups up to 1 day in advance. Cover and refrigerate. Garnish up to 1 hour before serving.

CHOCOLATE CUPS WITH STRAWBERRIES AND ORANGE CREME FRAICHE

MAKES 20
⅔ cup crème fraîche or sour cream
grated zest of 1 orange
20 bought mini chocolate cups
5 strawberries, sliced

Mix crème fraîche or sour cream and orange zest together. Use a teaspoon to fill chocolate cups with orange crème fraîche. Garnish with strawberry slices.

THINK AHEAD
Fill cups up to 1 day in advance. Cover and refrigerate. Garnish up to 1 hour before serving.

SOBA NOODLES WITH SESAME GINGER VINAIGRETTE IN SPOONS

MAKES 20

½ lb soba noodles
1 tbsp pickled ginger, finely chopped
2 tsp Chinese hot chilli sauce
4 tbsp rice wine vinegar
4 tbsp dark soy sauce
4 tbsp sesame oil
6 tbsp sunflower oil
2 tbsp sesame seeds

ESSENTIAL EQUIPMENT
20 Chinese or soup spoons

Bring a pan of water to the boil over medium heat and add the noodles. When the water returns to a boil, add 1 cup of cold water. Continue cooking until water returns to a boil again. Repeat this process 1 or 2 times until the noodles are tender to the bite, 5–7 minutes. Drain and cool noodles in cold water. Let stand in the colander for 5 minutes to drain well.
Combine noodles, ginger, chili sauce, vinegar, soy, and oils and stir to coat the noodles well.
Toast seeds in a dry pan over low heat until nutty and golden, 3 minutes. Divide noodles into 20 equal-sized portions. Twirl each noodle portion around a fork to make a nest. Transfer to spoons. Garnish with sesame seeds. Serve at room temperature.

THINK AHEAD
Cook and dress noodles in vinaigrette up to 1 day in advance. Cover and refrigerate. Return to room temperature before serving.

COOKS' NOTE
Adding cold water to the noodles as they cook checks overvigorous boiling to ensure that the noodles cook evenly.

FRAGRANT COCONUT SAFFRON SHRIMP IN SPOONS

MAKES 20

20 raw tiger shrimp, peeled
1 lemon grass stalk
1 shallot, finely chopped
½-inch piece fresh ginger, grated
1 garlic clove, finely chopped

pinch ground coriander
pinch saffron
1 tbsp sunflower oil
½ cup coconut milk
¼ tsp salt, ¼ tsp black pepper

ESSENTIAL EQUIPMENT
20 Chinese or soup spoons

With a small sharp knife, cut each shrimp almost in half lengthwise, leaving the tail end attached (see below, right).
Remove and discard the tough outer skin from the lemon grass and finely chop. In a nonmetallic bowl, toss lemon grass, shallots, ginger, garlic, spices, oil, and shrimp together to coat each shrimp well. Cover and refrigerate for 1 hour.
Remove shrimp and place lemon grass mixture in a pan over a low heat. Cook gently, stirring, until fragrant, 5 minutes. Add coconut milk, salt, and pepper. Bring slowly to a bowl over medium heat. Add shrimp and simmer slowly until they turn pink and lose their transparency, 3 minutes. Arrange 1 shrimp in each spoon. Drizzle with a little of the sauce just to coat. Serve warm.

COOKS' NOTE
For both of the recipes on this page choose spoons that sit well on a flat surface and are easy to pick up.

PASSION-FRUIT CURD TARTLETS

MAKES 20

5 passion fruit, halved
juice of ½ lemon
4 tbsp sugar
4 tbsp butter
1 egg, beaten
1 recipe baked pastry tartlets
  (see pages 136–137)
2 tsp powdered sugar for dusting

ESSENTIAL EQUIPMENT
small nonstick or heavy-bottomed saucepan

Scoop passion fruit pulp out of each half with a teaspoon. Combine passion-fruit pulp, lemon juice, and sugar in saucepan. Add butter and place over a low heat. Stir occasionally, until the butter has melted. Beat egg constantly, while gradually pouring in the hot passion fruit mixture, until well blended. Return mixture to the pan. Cook over low heat, stirring constantly, until thick and creamy, 10 minutes. Remove from the heat and continue stirring until cooled slightly. Cool completely. Divide curd among tartlets. Dust with powdered sugar to garnish. Serve chilled or at room temperature.

THINK AHEAD
Make curd up to 3 days in advance. Cover and refrigerate. Fill tartlets up to 1 hour before serving.

COOKS' NOTE
Make lime or pink grapefruit curd for a refreshing alternative. Use ⅔ cup lime or pink grapefruit juice and 1 tsp grated lime or pink grapefruit zest instead of the passion-fruit pulp and lemon juice.

CHERRY AND ALMOND FRANGIPANE TARTLETS

MAKES 20

2 tbsp butter, softened
2 tbsp sugar
¼ cup ground almonds
1 egg yolk
1 tbsp heavy cream
1 recipe baked pastry tartlets
  (see pages 136–137)
20 cherries (about 1 cup), pitted
2 tsp powdered sugar for dusting

Preheat oven to 350°F.
Combine butter, sugar, almonds, egg, and cream until well blended. Divide evenly among tartlets. Place 1 cherry on top of each tartlet. Bake until set and golden, 15 minutes. Cool completely. Dust with powdered sugar to garnish. Serve at room temperature.

THINK AHEAD
Bake filled tartlets up to 1 day in advance. Store in an airtight container at room temperature. Garnish just before serving.

COOKS' NOTE
Use canned sweet cherries when fresh cherries are out of season.

CITRUS GINGER CREAM TARTLETS

MAKES 20

grated zest and juice of 1 lime
grated zest and juice of 1 lemon
6 pieces preserved stem ginger, chopped
5 tbsp heavy cream
1 cup sweetened condensed milk
1 recipe baked pastry tartlets
  (see pages 136–137)

ESSENTIAL EQUIPMENT
piping bag fitted with large star tip

Place lime and lemon zest, ginger, cream, and condensed milk in a food processor or blender; pulse until combined. With the machine running, slowly pour in the lime and lemon juices until blended. Transfer to a bowl. Cover and refrigerate until set, 1 hour. Fill piping bag and pipe filling into the tartlets (see page 146). Garnish with ginger slices. Serve chilled or at room temperature.

THINK AHEAD
Fill tartlets up to 1 day in advance. Cover and refrigerate. Garnish up to 2 hours before serving.

SUMMER BERRY TARTLETS

1 recipe vanilla pastry cream (see page 144)
1 recipe baked pastry tartlets (see pages 136–37)
1⅔ cup summer berries: raspberries, halved
  strawberries, blackberries, or blueberries
2 tsp powdered sugar for dusting

ESSENTIAL EQUIPMENT
piping bag with large star tip

Fill piping bag with pastry cream (see page 146). Pipe into
tartlets. Arrange berries on top. Dust with powdered sugar.
Serve at room temperature.

THINK AHEAD
Assemble tartlets up to 3 hours in advance. Keep at room temperature.
Dust just before serving.

BITTERSWEET CHOCOLATE TARTLETS

MAKES 20
⅓ cup heavy cream
1 egg yolk
2½ oz bittersweet chocolate, broken into pieces
1 recipe baked pastry tartlets (see pages 136–37)
1 tbsp cocoa for dusting

Bring cream to a boil. Beat boiling cream into the egg yolk
in a separate bowl. Add chocolate and stir until melted and
smooth. Allow to cool until slightly thickened, 30 minutes.
Spoon into pastry tartlets. Leave to set at room temperature.
Dust with cocoa. Serve chilled or at room temperature.

THINK AHEAD
Make filling and assemble tartlets up to 3 hours in advance. Cover and
refrigerate. Dust just before serving.

COOKS' NOTE
The chocolate flavor in this recipe is unadulterated, so use the brand of
chocolate you like best. More or less bitter, depending on your preference.

CARAMELIZED LEMON TARTLETS

MAKES 20
1 egg, beaten
2 tbsp sugar
2 tbsp lemon juice, about 1 lemon
grated zest of 1 lemon
2 tbsp heavy cream
1 recipe baked pastry tartlets (see pages 136–37)
2 tbsp sugar to caramelize

Preheat oven to 375°F.
Beat eggs and sugar together until sugar dissolves. Whisk in
lemon juice, zest, and cream until just combined. Leave for
5 minutes. Skim any froth off the top. Pour lemon mixture into
baked tartlets. Bake until only just set, 5–8 minutes. Cool to
room temperature. Sprinkle tartlets with a thin layer of sugar.
Place tartlets under a preheated broiler as close to the heat as
possible until the sugar has colored, 1–2 minutes. Watch
constantly to avoid burning. Serve at room temperature.

THINK AHEAD
Bake filled tartlets up to 1 day in advance. Cover and refrigerate. Caramelize
tops up to 3 hours before serving.

ORIENTAL CHICKEN WITH SPICY PESTO TARTLETS

MAKES 20

1 boneless, skinless chicken breast

2 tbsp light soy sauce

1 tbsp rice vinegar

1 tbsp sesame oil

1 tbsp sunflower oil

FOR PESTO

1 cup cilantro leaves

10 mint leaves

1 green chili, seeded

1 scallion

1 tbsp roasted peanuts

1 tbsp sesame oil

1 recipe baked star-shaped sesame seed tartlets (see pages 136–37)

Place chicken in pan with cold water to cover. Bring to simmering over low heat. Simmer gently without boiling until cooked through, 7–10 minutes. Cool completely in cooking liquid. Drain and shred chicken. Toss chicken with soy sauce, vinegar, sesame and sunflower oils. Place cilantro, mint, chili, scallion, peanuts, and oil in a food processor or blender; pulse to thick paste. Fill tartlets with chicken and top with pesto. Serve at room temperature.

THINK AHEAD
Cook chicken up to 2 days in advance. Cover and refrigerate. Prepare pesto up to 3 days in advance. Cover and refrigerate. Fill tartlets up to 2 hours before serving.

RARE ROAST BEEF WITH WHOLEGRAIN CREME FRAICHE IN POPPY SEED TARTLETS

MAKES 20

½ lb rare roast beef slices

1 tbsp grainy mustard

6 tbsp crème fraîche or sour cream

1 recipe baked star-shaped poppy seed tartlets (see pages 136–37)

20 tarragon sprigs to garnish

Cut beef slices into 1-inch-wide strips. Stir mustard into crème fraîche or sour cream and divide among tartlets. Roll up beef slices and place on top of cream. Garnish with tarragon. Serve at room temperature.

THINK AHEAD
Make cream up to 1 day in advance. Fill tartlets up to 2 hours before serving

SHRIMP WITH GINGER MAYONNAISE IN CILANTRO TARTLETS

MAKES 20

6 tbsp mayonnaise (see page 142)

1 tsp finely chopped ginger

½ tsp turmeric

½ lb medium shrimp cooked and peeled

salt, cayenne pepper

1 fresh red chili, seeded

1 recipe baked star-shaped cilantro tartlets (see pages 136–37)

20 cilantro leaves to garnish

Combine mayonnaise with ginger and turmeric. Add shrimp then salt and pepper to taste. Cut chili into very fine julienne strips (see page 147). Divide shrimp mixture among tartlets. Garnish with chili and cilantro leaves. Serve at room temperature.

THINK AHEAD
Make filling up to 1 day in advance. Cover andrefrigerate. Fill tartlets up to 2 hours before serving.

FETA, OLIVE, AND ROSEMARY QUICHETTES

MAKES 20

½ cup crumbled feta cheese
1 egg yolk
3 tbsp heavy cream
black pepper
5 pitted black olives, quartered
20 rosemary sprigs to garnish
1 recipe baked pastry tartlets
  (see pages 136–37)

Preheat oven to 350°F. Divide feta among tartlets. Beat egg and cream together. Add pepper to taste. Spoon egg mixture into tartlets. Top with olive quarters and rosemary sprigs. Bake until golden and set, 7 minutes. Serve warm.

THINK AHEAD
Bake up to 2 days in advance. Store in an airtight container in the refrigerator. Warm through in preheated 300°F oven for 10 minutes.

COOKS' NOTE
Try a variety of cheeses and herbs. Our favorites are brie and thyme or goat's cheese and oregano.

BLUE CHEESE, MASCARPONE, AND RED ONION CONFIT QUICHETTES

MAKES 20

1 recipe baked rosemary tartlets
  (see pages 136–37)
2 tbsp butter
1 medium red onion, finely sliced
¼ tsp salt
1 tbsp brown sugar
black pepper
½ cup crumbled Gorgonzola cheese
3 tbsp mascarpone cheese
1 egg yolk

Preheat oven to 350°F.
Melt butter in a frying pan. Stir in onions. Sprinkle with salt and sugar. Cook gently, stirring occasionally, until soft and dark, 30 minutes. Add salt and pepper to taste. Divide among baked tartlet cases. Crumble Gorgonzola over tartlets. Beat mascarpone and egg until combined. Spoon into tartlets. Bake until golden, 7 minutes. Serve warm.

THINK AHEAD
Bake up to 2 days in advance. Store in an airtight container in the refrigerator. Warm through in preheated 300°F oven for 10 minutes.

PORTOBELLO MUSHROOM AND HOLLANDAISE TARTLETS

MAKES 20

2 tbsp butter
1 shallot, finely chopped
2½ cups chopped portobello mushrooms
1 tbsp cream cheese
2 tbsp lemon juice
salt, black pepper
1 recipe lemon hollandaise (see page 143)
1 recipe baked pastry tartlets
  (see pages 136–37)
6 basil leaves, cut into chiffonade
  (see below, right)

Preheat oven to 400°F.
Heat butter in a skillet. Add shallots and mushrooms. Stir fry over high heat until softened, 5 minutes. Cool slightly. Place mushroom mixture, cream cheese, and lemon in a food processor or blender; pulse to a rough purée. Add salt and pepper to taste. Divide mushroom mixture among tartlets. Put 1 tsp hollandaise on top; heat through in oven for 5 minutes. Sprinkle with basil. Serve warm.

THINK AHEAD
Make mushroom mixture up to 3 days in advance. Cover and refrigerate. Fill tartlets up to 2 hours before serving. Store at room temperature.

COOKS' NOTE
If you are short of time, use store-bought hollandaise.

MAKING BASIL CHIFFONADE
Stack basil leaves and roll them together tightly. Slice across roll to make very fine strips.

EGG, CAPER, AND CRESS FINGER SANDWICHES

MAKES 30
4 medium eggs
1 tbsp finely chopped drained capers
½ cup watercress, finely chopped
4 tbsp mayonnaise
salt, black pepper
3 tbsp butter, softened
10 medium slices white bread

Place the eggs in a pan of cold water. Bring water to a boil, then reduce heat and simmer for 8 minutes. Drain and cool eggs completely in cold water. Peel and chop eggs. Combine eggs, capers, watercress, and mayonnaise. Add salt and pepper to taste. Spread butter, then egg mayonnaise evenly over 5 bread slices. Top with remaining bread. Cut off crusts using a serrated knife and discard. Cut each sandwich in half, then cut each half into 3 fingers about 1½ inches wide. Serve chilled or at room temperature.

THINK AHEAD
Make sandwiches up to 1 day in advance, but do not remove crusts or cut. Cover with plastic wrap and refrigerate. Cut sandwiches up to 3 hours in advance. Cover and keep at room temperature.

RARE ROAST BEEF AND HORSERADISH MAYONNAISE FINGER SANDWICHES

2 tbsp mayonnaise (see page 142)
2 tsp horseradish sauce
10 medium slices whole-wheat bread
6oz thinly sliced rare roast beef
3 tbsp butter, softened

Combine mayonnaise and horseradish. Spread 5 bread slices evenly with horseradish-mayonnaise mixture. Top with roast beef. Spread butter evenly over remaining bread slices. Top beef with bread slices buttered-side down. Cut off crusts using a serrated knife and discard. Cut each sandwich in half, then cut each half into 3 fingers about 1½ inches wide. Serve chilled or at room temperature.

THINK AHEAD
Make sandwiches up to 1 day in advance, but do not remove crusts or cut. Cover and refrigerate. Cut sandwiches up to 3 hours in advance.

SMOKED SALMON AND CHIVE CREAM FINGER SANDWICHES

MAKES 30
¾ cup cream cheese
5 tbsp finely chopped chives
grated zest of ½ lemon
1 tbsp lemon juice
10 medium slices whole-wheat bread
½ lb smoked salmon slices
black pepper
3 tbsp butter, softened

Combine cream cheese, chives, lemon juice, and zest. Spread mixture evenly over 5 bread slices. Top with smoked salmon and sprinkle with black pepper. Spread butter evenly over remaining bread slices. Top salmon with bread slices buttered-side down. Cut off crusts using a serrated knife and discard. Cut each sandwich in half, then cut each half into 3 fingers about 1½-inches wide. Serve chilled or at room temperature.

THINK AHEAD
Make sandwiches up to 1 day in advance, but do not remove crusts or cut. Cover with plastic wrap and refrigerate. Cut sandwiches up to 3 hours in advance.

COOK'S NOTE
You can make circle sandwiches using a 1½-inch plain pastry cutter to stamp out 4 rounds from each sandwich.

CUCUMBER AND CHERVIL FINGER SANDWICHES

MAKES 30
½ cucumber, peeled and thinly sliced
½ tsp salt
6 tbsp butter, softened
10 medium slices white bread
white pepper
2 tbsp finely chopped chervil

Place cucumber slices in a colander. Sprinkle evenly with salt. Cover and let stand for 1 hour. Pat cucumber dry with paper towels. Spread butter evenly over all bread slices. Top 5 bread slices with cucumber. Sprinkle over white pepper and chervil. Top cucumber with remaining bread slices. Cut off crusts using a serrated knife and discard. Cut each sandwich in half, then cut each half into 3 fingers about 1½-inches wide. Serve chilled or at room temperature.

THINK AHEAD
Make sandwiches up to 8 hours in advance, but do not remove crusts or cut. Cover and refrigerate. Cut sandwiches up to 3 hours in advance.

MINI CROQUE MONSIEUR

MAKES 20
10 medium white bread slices
5 ham slices
2¼ cups grated Gruyère cheese

Preheat oven to 400°F.
Top 5 bread slices with one slice ham each. Sprinkle half the cheese over the five slices. Press the remaining bread slices on top to make sandwiches. Place on a baking sheet. Sprinkle the remaining cheese across the top of the sandwiches. Bake until cheese is golden and melted, 10 minutes. Cool slightly. Cut off the crusts with a serrated knife. Cut each sandwich into 4 squares. Serve warm.

CROQUE MONSIEUR VARIATION
MINI CROQUE MADAME

Use 1⅛ cups grated Gruyère cheese instead of 2¼ cups. Fill sandwiches as directed but do not top with cheese. Bake until bread is toasted, 10 minutes. Cut sandwiches as directed. Fry 20 quail eggs in 2 tbsp butter. Top each sandwich square with a quail egg. Sprinkle over salt and pepper and serve immediately.

THINK AHEAD
Assemble sandwiches up to 1 day in advance. Cover and refrigerate. Bake just before serving.

COOKS' NOTE
When making the croque madame, use the tip of a small sharp knife to crack open the quail eggs.

THE TECHNIQUES

A LITTLE EXTRA TIME AND EFFORT

FOR A SPECIAL OCCASION,

FOR FRIENDS, FOR FAMILY –

IT'S WORTH IT.

SHORT-CRUST PASTRY

MAKES 10oz
1½ cup all-purpose flour, sifted
¼ tsp salt
1½ tsp sugar
6 tbsp chilled butter, cubed
1 egg yolk
2 tbsp water

Place flour, salt, sugar, and butter in a bowl. Also add any flavoring, if using, to the bowl. With 2 knives, cut the butter into the dry ingredients until the mixture resembles fine crumbs (see near right).

Add egg yolk. Mix with a wooden spoon to bring ingredients together. Add remaining water as necessary, ½ tbsp at a time, until the pastry begins to come together (see far right). Bring the pastry together completely with your hands. Turn out of bowl onto a lightly floured surface. Knead briefly to make a smooth round.

THINK AHEAD
Make pastry up to 2 days in advance. Wrap in plastic wrap and refrigerate. Return to room temperature before rolling out. Alternatively, make pastry and freeze up to 1 month in advance. Defrost overnight in refrigerator.

COOKS' NOTE
To ensure perfect pastry, the ingredients should be very cold. To guarantee the best results, place butter and flour in the freezer for 5 minutes before you begin.
As a general rule we do not recommend chilling the pastry, but if the weather is hot or the pastry has been overhandled, wrap in plastic wrap and refrigerate for 30 minutes before rolling out.

Cut in the butter with 2 knives.　　　　　Add the water ½ tbsp at a time.

FLAVORED SHORT-CRUST PASTRY VARIATIONS

Add the specified flavoring to the dry ingredients with the chilled butter. The flavoring ingredient will contribute extra moisture to the pastry, so you may need less liquid than usual to bind the pastry together.

CILANTRO PASTRY
Follow short-crust pastry recipe, adding 1 tbsp finely chopped cilantro to the dry ingredients.

POPPY-SEED PASTRY
Follow short-crust pastry recipe, adding 1 tsp poppy seeds to the dry ingredients.

ROSEMARY PASTRY
Follow short-crust pastry recipe, adding 1 tsp finely chopped rosemary leaves to the dry ingredients.

SESAME PASTRY
Follow short-crust pastry recipe, adding 1 tsp sesame seeds to the dry ingredients.

USING A MACHINE

Follow recipe for short-crust pastry. Place flour, salt, sugar, and butter, with any flavoring, if using, in a food processor; pulse until mixture resembles fine crumbs. Add egg yolk; pulse until the pastry forms a ball. Add more water as necessary, ½ tbsp at a time. Turn pastry out of the machine onto a lightly floured surface and knead briefly by hand to make a smooth round.

BAKING PASTRY TARTLETS

MAKES 20

1 recipe unbaked short-crust pastry (see page 136)

ESSENTIAL EQUIPMENT

20 - 1¾-inch plain or fluted tartlet tins and
1 - 2-inch plain or fluted pastry cutter

ALTERNATIVELY

2 - 12-cup mini-muffin pans and
1 - 2½-inch plain or fluted pastry cutter

Baking beans (store-bought ceramic beans, or alternatively, dried beans)

Preheat oven to 400°F.
On a lightly floured surface, roll out pastry to a ⅛-inch thickness. Cut out 20 rounds with the appropriate pastry cutter according to the type of tin specified by the recipe. Use the cut pastry rounds to line the tins (see below, left). Prick the base of each tartlet once with a fork. Refrigerate for 30 minutes before baking.

Fold a piece of baking parchment paper about 12 inches long into small squares about 3 x 3 inches. Cut the folded paper along the folded ends with scissors. Separate paper to make about 21 paper squares. Do not discard paper liners after using, since they can be used again

Press a baking parchment paper square into each pastry case. Fill paper with baking beans (see below, center right). Bake tartlets until firm, 10 minutes. Remove paper and beans. Continue baking until crisp and golden, 10 minutes. Cool slightly, then transfer to a wire rack to finish cooling.

THINK AHEAD
Line tartlet tins up to 1 day in advance. Cover and refrigerate. Bake tartlets up to 3 days in advance. Store in an airtight container at room temperature.

COOKS' NOTES
Roll out pastry between 2 large pieces of plastic wrap to prevent pastry from cracking.
Lining the unbaked tartlets with paper and beans helps the pastry keep its shape when baked. If you are an experienced pastry maker and are confident that your pastry won't shrink, place the pastry tartlets in the freezer until solid and bake unlined from frozen.

Bake tartlets filled with paper and beans to prevent pastry from shrinking in the oven.

MAKING STAR-SHAPED TARTLETS

Follow method for rolling out pastry given in the instructions above. Cut out 20 rounds with a 3¼-inch-star-shaped pastry cutter. Butter 2 - 12-cup mini muffin pans and line each muffin cup with one star-shaped piece of pastry dough. Follow method for baking pastry (see above).

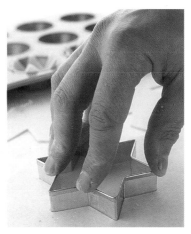

Cut out the stars.

Line the tartlet tins with the pastry rounds.

CHOUX PASTRY

MAKES 1lb

1 cup all-purpose flour, sifted
¾ cup water
½ tsp salt
3 tbsp butter
3 eggs

Place water, salt, and butter in a an over medium heat. Bring just to a boil and remove from the heat. Add the flour to the pan, stirring constantly with a wooden spoon, until combined (see right). Return the pan to the heat and beat until the mixture is smooth and pulls away from the sides of the pan, 1 minute.

Remove from the heat and beat in the eggs, one at a time, making sure that each egg is thoroughly incorporated before adding the next one. Beat until the mixture is smooth, glossy, and slightly sticky (see bottom right).

Add the flour and stir constantly with a wooden spoon until combined.

Remove from the heat and add the eggs one at a time.

USING A MACHINE

We recommend using a food processor only for making choux pastry in large quantities (doubling or tripling the quantities given above). Make choux pastry as directed but transfer to a food processor before adding the eggs. While the machine is running, add eggs one at a time until the mixture is smooth, glossy, and slightly sticky.

CHOUX PUFFS

MAKES 35

1 recipe choux pastry (see page 138)

ESSENTIAL EQUIPMENT

2 tablespoons or a piping bag fitted with a large plain tip

Preheat oven to 350°F.

Use the tips of the 2 tablespoons to place small walnut-sized spoonfuls of choux pastry, ¾ inch apart, onto a buttered baking sheet (see right). Bake until light, crisp and golden, 35 minutes. Cool on a wire rack.

Alternatively, fill the piping bag with the choux pastry (see page 146) and pipe small walnut-sized mounds, ¾ inch apart, onto a buttered baking sheet. Bake until light, crisp and golden, 35 minutes. Cool on a wire rack.

THINK AHEAD
Bake choux puffs up to 3 days in advance. Store in an airtight container at room temperature. Alternatively, freeze baked choux puffs up to 1 month in advance. Defrost overnight in refrigerator. Crisp in a preheated 400°F oven for 3 minutes.

COOKS' NOTE
Underbaked puffs do not keep, and turn soggy when filled. It is essential to check one puff for doneness before removing the entire baking sheet from the oven. Split open one puff: the interior must be hollow and completely dry. Continue baking if necessary until the puffs are completely dry.

Use the tips of 2 tablespoons to shape puffs.

Alternatively, use a piping bag.

CHOUX MINI ECLAIRS

MAKES 30

1 recipe choux pastry (see page 138)

ESSENTIAL EQUIPMENT
piping bag fitted with a large plain tip

Preheat oven to 350°F.
Fill a piping bag with choux pastry (see page 146). Pipe out 30 spiral-shaped strips about 2 inches long onto a buttered baking sheet. Leave 1½ inches between each strip to allow for expansion in the oven. Bake until light, crisp and golden, 35 minutes. Cool on a wire rack.

BREAD DOUGH

MAKES ¾ lb
1¾ cup plus 2 tbsp bread flour
1 tsp salt
⅔ cup warm water
1 tsp olive oil
1 tsp dried yeast

Place the flour in a bowl and make a well in the center. Sprinkle the salt along the raised edge of the flour. Pour the water with the oil into the well. Sprinkle the yeast over the liquid. Let stand for 5 minutes; stir to dissolve. Draw in the flour from the sides of the bowl with a spoon (see top right), and mix to make a rough, sticky dough.

Turn out dough onto a lightly floured surface. Use the heel of one hand to gently push the dough away from you. At the same time, use your other hand to rotate the dough slightly toward you, guiding it around in a circle (see center right). Repeat these kneading actions until the dough is smooth, shiny, and elastic, 10 minutes.

Put the dough in a clean, oiled bowl and cover with a dish towel (see opposite, bottom). Let rise until doubled in size, about 1½ hours. Deflate the dough by pressing down with the palm of your hand. The dough is now ready to be shaped.

THINK AHEAD
Make and knead 12 hours in advance. Cover and let rise in refrigerator overnight. Let stand at room temperature for 30 minutes before shaping. Shape and bake according to the recipe.

COOKS' NOTE
The quantity of liquid required will often vary according to the type of flour used, as well as the level of humidity and temperature on the day of breadmaking. It is best to err on the side of making a dough too soft rather than too dry. Add extra water after drawing in the flour to form dough, as necessary, 1 tbsp at a time.

Draw in the flour from the sides of the bowl.

Knead the dough until smooth and elastic.

Cover the dough with a dish towel to rise.

USING A MACHINE
Follow recipe and method for bread dough, but place ingredients, after they have been mixed to a rough dough, into the bowl of a heavy-duty mixer fitted with a dough hook. To knead, set the mixer at low speed for 10 minutes.
Alternatively, use the bowl of a food processor fitted with a plastic dough blade. To knead, use the pulse button for 30 seconds at a time, until dough is smooth and elastic, 4 minutes.

VANILLA MERINGUE

MAKES 1¼ cups

2 egg whites at room temperature
½ cup plus 2 tbsp sugar
½ tsp vanilla extract

Put the egg whites in a large, clean bowl and whisk until the meringue holds soft peaks (see near right).

Add the sugar, 1 tbsp at a time, whisking well after each addition (see far right). Continue whisking until the whites are stiff and glossy. Fold in vanilla with a rubber spatula and any additional flavoring, if using, according to the instructions given for the flavor variations (see below).

COOKS' NOTE
Make sure the bowl is completely grease-free or your whites will not stiffen. If in doubt, wipe with paper towels dipped in vinegar before you begin.

A daring, but effective, way to check if the whites are sufficiently stiff is to hold the bowl upside down: the meringue should not fall out!

FLAVORED MERINGUE VARIATIONS
Add the flavoring to the meringue with the vanilla. Fold in with a spatula until evenly combined.

CHOCOLATE MERINGUE
Fold in 1 tsp sifted cocoa powder with the vanilla.

HAZELNUT MERINGUE
Fold in 2 tbsp ground blanched hazelnuts with the vanilla.

MUSCAVADO MERINGUE
Fold in 1 tbsp dark brown sugar with the vanilla.

PISTACHIO MERINGUE
Fold in 1 tbsp chopped unsalted pistachios with the vanilla.

Whisk egg whites to soft peaks.   Add sugar 1 tbsp at a time.

VANILLA MERINGUE KISSES

MAKES 40

1 recipe unbaked vanilla meringue (see left)

ESSENTIAL EQUIPMENT
piping bag fitted with large star tip

Preheat oven to 250°F. Fill piping bag with meringue (see page 146). Pipe 40 meringue rosettes, 1 inch apart, on to baking parchment-lined baking sheets. Bake until crisp and dry, 1 hour. Cool completely before removing from the baking sheet.

THINK AHEAD
Bake up to 1 week in advance. Store in an airtight container at room temperature.

Pipe kisses 1 inch apart.

MINI MERINGUES

MAKES 20

1 recipe unbaked vanilla meringue (see left)

Preheat oven to 350°F. Use the tip of two teaspoons to place small walnut-sized spoonfuls of meringue, 1 inch apart, onto parchment-lined baking sheets. Make an indentation in the center of each mini meringue with the back of one teaspoon. Bake for 5 minutes, then turn the oven temperature down to 250°F. Continue baking until firm to the touch, 20 minutes.
Cool the mini meringues completely before removing them from the baking sheet.

THINK AHEAD
Bake up to 2 days in advance.
Store in an airtight container at room temperature.

Shape meringue with the back of a teaspoon.

MAYONNAISE

MAKES 1½ cups

2 egg yolks
1 tsp creamy Dijon mustard
1 tbsp red wine vinegar
½ tsp salt
pinch black pepper
1 tsp sugar
1¼ cups sunflower oil
black pepper

ESSENTIAL EQUIPMENT
wire whisk

Make sure that all the ingredients are at room temperature before you begin. Set a deep bowl on a cloth to prevent it from slipping as you whisk. Whisk the egg yolks, mustard, vinegar, salt, pepper, and sugar together in a bowl until thick and creamy, 1 minute (see near right).

Place the oil in a jug. Whisk in the oil a drop at a time until the mixture thickens. Add the remaining oil in a thin, steady stream, whisking constantly until thick and glossy (see far right). Whisk in any flavoring, if using, according to the recipe variations. Adjust seasoning, adding more mustard, vinegar, salt, pepper, or sugar to taste.

THINK AHEAD
Make mayonnaise up to 3 days in advance. Cover and refrigerate. Return to room temperature before stirring to prevent the mayonnaise from separating.

COOKS' NOTE
If the ingredients are too cold or the oil is added too quickly, the mayonnaise may separate. Don't throw it away! Combine 1 tsp vinegar and 1 tsp creamy Dijon mustard in a clean bowl. Whisk in the separated mayonnaise drop by drop until the mixture reemulsifies.

SAFETY WARNING ON RAW EGGS
Because of the potential risk of salmonella, pregnant women, young children, and anyone with a weakened immune system should avoid eating raw eggs. Make sure you use only the freshest (preferably organic) eggs, and if in doubt, substitute store-bought mayonnaise (see right).

Whisk the yolks until thick and creamy.

Add the oil in a steady stream.

FLAVORED MAYONNAISE VARIATIONS
Whisk flavouring into the finished mayonnaise. Make sure that the flavoring and mayonnaise are at room temperature before you begin.

LEMON MAYONNAISE
Whisk 1 tbsp lemon juice into 1 recipe mayonnaise.

LEMON AIOLI
Crush 2 garlic cloves. Whisk crushed garlic into 1 recipe lemon mayonnaise (see variation above).

LIGHT LEMON MAYONNAISE
Whisk 2 tbsp warm water into 1 recipe lemon mayonnaise (see above) to lighten flavor, color, and consistency.

USING STORE-BOUGHT MAYONNAISE
Use store-bought mayonnaise when in need of a time saving shortcut or if health concerns are an issue for you. Seek out a good quality whole-egg brand of mayonnaise and freshen the flavor by whisking in creamy Dijon mustard, sugar, and red-wine vinegar or lemon juice to taste.

USING A MACHINE
Follow recipe for mayonnaise. Place the egg yolks, mustard, vinegar, salt, pepper, and sugar with 3 tbsp of the oil in a blender or food processor; process until blended, 10 seconds. While the machine is running, pour in the remaining oil in a thin, steady stream, until the mixture emulsifies and becomes thick and glossy. Pulse in any flavoring, if using. Adjust seasoning, adding more mustard, vinegar, salt, pepper, or sugar to taste.

COOKS' NOTE
If using a food processor, depending on its capacity, you may need to stop the machine at intervals to scrape down the sides and over the base of the bowl with a spatula.

LEMON HOLLANDAISE

MAKES ¾ cup
4 tbsp butter
2 tbsp water
2 egg yolks
salt and white pepper
juice of ½ lemon

Melt the butter, then skim the froth from the surface with a spoon. Let cool until lukewarm. Place a heatproof bowl over a pan of simmering water set on low heat. Make sure the base of the bowl is not in direct contact with the hot water. Place water and yolks with a pinch each salt and pepper in the bowl. Whisk the ingredients to a light and frothy mixture that holds the trail of the whisk, 3 minutes (see near right). Remove the pan from the heat.

Whisk in butter, a little at a time, whisking vigorously after each addition, until the mixture emulsifies and becomes thick and creamy (see far right). Gradually whisk in the lemon juice. Adjust seasoning, adding more salt, pepper, or lemon juice to taste.

THINK AHEAD
Make hollandaise up to 30 minutes in advance. Keep warm in a bowl over a pan of hot water placed off the heat. Alternatively, make hollandaise up to 2 days in advance. Cover and refrigerate. Place in a heatproof bowl over a pan of simmering water set over low heat. Make sure the base of the bowl is not in direct contact with the water. Warm through, whisking occasionally, until lukewarm, 10 minutes.

COOKS' NOTE
If the butter is added too quickly, the hollandaise may separate. Don't throw it away! Combine 1 tbsp water and 1 egg yolk in a clean bowl over a pan of simmering water set on a low heat. Make sure the base of the bowl is not in contact with the water. Whisk to a light and frothy mixture that holds that trail of the whisk, 3 minutes. Remove the pan from the heat. Whisk in the separated hollandaise, a little at a time, whisking vigorously after each addition, until the mixture reemulsifies.

Whisk the water and egg yolks to a light, frothy mixture.

Add the butter a little at a time.

SAUCE BEARNAISE

Place 3 tbsp red-wine vinegar, 6 peppercorns, 1 finely chopped shallot, and 1 sprig each tarragon and chervil in a small pan. Bring the ingredients to a boil over medium heat and continue cooking until the liquid is reduced to 1 tbsp. Cool and strain. Now follow the recipe for hollandaise, omitting the lemon juice. Place the reduction in a bowl with the water, egg yolks, salt, and pepper and follow the recipe method. Stir in 1 tsp each of finely chopped tarragon and chervil after the butter has been added. Adjust seasoning, adding more salt and pepper to taste.

USING A MACHINE

Follow recipe for lemon hollandaise. Place egg yolks, salt, and pepper in a food processor or blender. Bring butter, water, and lemon juice to simmering point in a small pan. While the machine is running, pour in the hot butter mixture in a slow, steady stream until the mixture emulsifies and becomes thick and creamy. Adjust seasoning, adding more salt, pepper, or lemon juice to taste.

COOKS' NOTE
If using a food processor, depending on its capacity, you may need to stop the machine at intervals to scrape down the sides and over the base of the bowl with a spatula.

VANILLA PASTRY CREAM

MAKES ¾ cup

2 eggs
2 tbsp sugar
2 tsp all-purpose flour
½ cup milk
¼ tsp vanilla extract

Place the eggs and sugar in a bowl. Whisk until thick and light, 2 minutes. Add the flour and continue whisking until smooth (see top, near right).

In a small heavy-bottomed saucepan, bring the milk just to a boil over medium heat. Pour the boiling milk into the egg mixture, while whisking constantly until the mixture is completely smooth (see top, far right). Pour the mixture through a strainer into a pan and place over medium heat.

Cook the strained pastry cream until very thick, stirring constantly, 2 minutes (see center, near right). Reduce heat to low and cook, stirring constantly, until pastry cream no longer tastes of raw flour, 2 minutes. Stir in vanilla with any additional flavoring, if using, according to the recipe variation (see page 145).

Transfer pastry cream to a bowl to cool. Press waxed paper directly onto the surface of the pastry cream to stop a skin from forming (see center, far right).

THINK AHEAD
Make pastry cream up to 2 days in advance. Cover and refrigerate.

COOKS' NOTE
Don't worry if lumps form as the pastry cream cooks; continue cooking. After removing from the heat simply push the cooked pastry cream through a strainer to eliminate any lumps. Be sure to allow the pastry cream to cool completely before chilling. If it is not completely cold when refrigerated, the steam will condense and form watery puddles on the surface of the cream.

Add the flour and whisk until smooth.

Whisk constantly while adding the milk to the egg.

Cook the pastry cream until very thick.

Cover with waxed paper to cool.

WHIPPING CREAM

For whipping, cream must contain a minimum of 30% butterfat.

Make sure the cream, bowl, and whisk are well chilled before whipping: place in the refrigerator for 30 minutes or in the freezer for 10 minutes before you begin. Pour the cream into a bowl and whisk until it starts to thicken. Continue whisking until the cream is light and just holds a soft peak when the whisk is lifted. If the recipe requires stiff peaks, continue whisking until the cream stands up when the whisk is removed, about 1 minute more.

Whisk cream until it holds soft peaks. Add sugar and continue whisking until the cream restiffens to soft or stiff peaks, 1–2 minutes.

THINK AHEAD
Make whipped cream up to 4 hours in advance. Cover and refrigerate.

COOKS' NOTE
If your cream begins to look granular and yellowish as you are whisking, you have over whipped it. To remedy, gently fold in a little extra cream, 1 tbsp at a time, to bring it back to a smooth, silky texture.

Whisk until cream holds soft peaks.

Add sugar to whipped cream and whisk to restiffen.

FLAVOURED PASTRY CREAM VARIATION

CHOCOLATE PASTRY CREAM

Follow the recipe and method for vanilla pastry cream. Melt 3½oz bittersweet chocolate (see right). Stir melted chocolate into the pastry cream with the vanilla until thoroughly combined and smooth in texture.

MAKING CARAMEL

Place sugar and water in a heavy-bottomed pan over a low heat. Stir constantly with a wooden spoon. Completely dissolve the sugar before allowing the liquid to come to a boil. Raise the heat to medium and bring the syrup to a boil. Do not stir the syrup. Boil rapidly until the syrup starts to brown around the edge of the pan. Lower the heat and continue cooking, swirling the pan once or twice so that the caramel colors evenly. Remove the pan from the heat shortly before the caramel reaches the desired color since it will continue to cook from the heat of the pan.

COOKS' NOTE
Once the syrup has boiled, do not stir because this might cause crystallization. If your caramel is coloring too fast, stop it from cooking by plunging the base of the pan in to a bowl of cold water. If it sets too hard, warm it gently through in the pan over a low heat until it melts, being careful not to let it boil or to continue to cook further.

MELTING CHOCOLATE

Chocolate should be melted gently and slowly since it will scorch if overheated.

Break chocolate into small pieces. Place in a heatproof bowl over a pan of hot, but not simmering, water set over a very low heat. Make sure the bottom of the bowl is not in contact with the water. Once the chocolate starts to melt, stir frequently. When about half the chocolate has melted, remove the pan from the heat and stir constantly until smooth, glossy, and completely melted.

COOKS' NOTE
Make sure the bowl fits snugly over the pan. If any steam escapes from the simmering water below and falls onto the chocolate as it melts, the chocolate may suddenly become rough, stiff, and lumpy. If this should happen, remove the chocolate from the heat immediately and stir in sunflower oil, 1 tsp at a time, until the chocolate becomes smooth again.

Light caramel is pale gold in color and is used for coating pastries.

Dark caramel is dark golden brown in color and is used for lining molds.

Once the chocolate begins to melt, remove from the heat and stir constantly until it is completely melted.

PREPARE THE PIPING BAG
Make sure the tip is fitted securely, then twist the bag above the tip to prevent leakage while filling.

FILL THE BAG
Fold the top of the bag over your hand to form a collar; spoon in the filling.

TWIST THE BAG TO PIPE
Twist the top of the bag until the filling is visible in the tip, to clear any air pockets before you begin.

MAKING A PAPER PIPING BAG

Fold a 9½-inch square of baking parchment in half diagonally and cut along the fold (see above). Bring one point of the triangle to the center to form a cone (see top right).

Wrap the remaining point of the triangle around to meet the other two points. Pull all 3 points tightly together to create a sharp point and fold flap inside (see bottom right). Crease the flap to hold the shape of the cone together.

PIPING, TOPPING, OR FILLING

Hold the piping bag in a vertical position and exert pressure on the bag with the fingers and palm of one hand to force out the filling. Guide the tip with the other hand. Exert a small amount of pressure on the bag to make a small rosette for topping.

Apply additional pressure to make a large rosette for filling. Lift the tip quickly to finish the rosette neatly.

CUTTING INTO JULIENNE STRIPS

Cut vegetable into very thin slices, about ⅛-inch thick. Cut the stacked slices into thin even-sized strips the size of matchsticks. To save time, stack the slices a few at a time before cutting into strips.

PEELING TOMATOES

Cut a small cross on the bottom of each tomato. Drop tomatoes into boiling water. Remove when you see the edges of each cross begin to loosen, 10–20 seconds, depending on the ripeness. Drain, then immerse in cold water. Peel off the loosened skins, using the tip of a knife.

SEEDING TOMATOES

Cut tomatoes into quarters. With a sharp knife, cut out seeds and core.

Seeding tomatoes is crucial in many recipes because the seeds exude juice and may make fresh salsas and garnishes watery.

CUTTING INTO FINE DICE

Cut the vegetable into thin, even slices. Stack the slices a few at a time. Cut the stack lengthwise to make equal-sized strips. Cut across to make an even-sized dice.

GRILLING AND PEELING PEPPERS

Roast pepper quarters skin side up under a hot broiler until charred and wrinkled, 5–10 minutes. Place in a plastic bag or a bowl with a plate on top and let stand until cool. The steam released by the peppers as they cool will loosen the skin. Uncover cooled peppers. Peel off the charred skin, using the tip of a small knife. Scrape rather than rinse off any remaining bits of skin. Rinsing the pepper will wash away the roasted flavor.

PEELING CITRUS FRUIT

Cut a thick slice from both ends to expose flesh. Stand upright and cut away peel and white pith, following the curve of the fruit.

SEGMENTING CITRUS FRUIT

Hold peeled fruit in one hand. Use the tip of the knife to cut down both sides of one white membrane to release segment.

MAKING HERB SPRIGS

Select only the freshest, greenest leaves when making herb sprigs for garnishing. Strip the leaves from the stalks and divide any larger sprigs into smaller pieces.

MAKING EDIBLE SKEWERS

Use edible skewers to add extra flavor to skewered foods. Some ideas used in the recipe section are illustrated here. Bay and thyme stalks are not shown, but also make effective skewers when their stems are stiff and thick enough to hold food.

LEMON GRASS SKEWERS

Remove and discard the tough outer skin from the lemon grass stalks. Cut in half lengthwise, keeping the stalks attached by the root. Cut into 4-inch lengths to use for skewers.

ASSEMBLING A WRAP

ROLLING UP THE FILLING

Place the wrap base on a piece of plastic wrap and cover with the filling. Use the plastic wrap underneath to help you as you carefully roll up the base around the filling as tightly as possible.

SUGARCANE STICKS

If using fresh sugarcane, peel with a vegetable peeler and trim to 4-inch lengths. Cut each sugarcane piece lengthwise into ¼-inch-thick slices. Cut slices into ¼-inch strips.

ROSEMARY SKEWERS

Strip the leaves from the stalks. Leave just a few leaves at one end. Sharpen the other end with a sharp knife to make threading food onto the skewer easier.

SECURING THE ROLL

Twist each end of plastic wrap tightly to secure and shape the roll.

MAKING PARMESAN SHAVINGS

MAKING AN INDENTATION
Cut out a slightly curved indent from the longest side of the piece of cheese with a sharp knife.

SHAVING THE PARMESAN
Use a vegetable peeler to shave curls from the indentation.

COVERING AIRTIGHT

Always press plastic wrap against the surface of foods to keep out as much air as possible. The oxygen in the air increases the spoilage and discoloration of many foods, such as avocado. Protecting food from the oxidizing properties of air will keep food looking and tasting fresher longer.

FREEZING UNBAKED ITEMS

To freeze unbaked items, spread out on a baking sheet and place in freezer uncovered until hard, 30 minutes. Once the items are frozen, pack into plastic freezer bags or an airtight container and return to the freezer. Remember to label items clearly for easier retrieval.

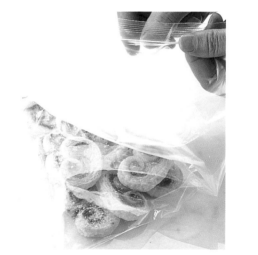

SEALING AIRTIGHT

Before sealing, expel all the air to make storage bags airtight. Resealable plastic bags are ideal for storing both wet and dry foods. Resealable plastic bags are also useful for marinating. They allow the marinade to be evenly distributed around the ingredients.

HOT-WEATHER COOKING

When planning a menu for hot weather, choose recipes that are fresh, light, and simple to prepare. Not only do rich, creamy foods require cool temperatures for storage if made ahead, but they tend to be less popular in the warmer months. We advise starting as early in the day as possible, when the temperature is coolest. Do not attempt too many jobs at a time. Get one recipe finished and immediately place in a storage container in the refrigerator or in another cool place. Coolers with ice packs are extremely useful in hot weather. They provide additional and portable refrigeration, especially when entertaining away from the house. Be careful to keep all food out of direct sunlight, both when storing and serving. For outdoor entertaining, find a shady, sheltered spot—and make sure it will still be in the shade during the hours you plan to entertain.

STORING IN LAYERS

Cooked pancakes and fritters, and raw pastries and doughs, are moist and may stick together if packed too tightly. Store in single layers in an airtight container with waxed paper or paper towels placed in between the layers to keep items separated.

THE PARTY

PLAN AHEAD,
CHOOSE A MENU WITH VARIETY,
PRESENT WITH SIMPLICITY AND STYLE;
YOU ARE SET FOR SUCCESS.

THE PLAN

THE MENU

The most crucial part of good menu composition is to include a variety of tastes, textures, aromas, and colors. Try to create a menu with contrasts. Choose a variety of hors d'oeuvres that will give your guests a balance of sweet, sharp, spicy, salty, and sour flavors. Remember that hors d'oeuvres should always be a small bite with a big flavor. Here are a few things to consider when planning your menu.

• Never attempt a menu with all brand new recipes. Experiment with unfamiliar recipes before the day of the party. Be sure to mix in a few tried and tested favorites.

• Let the seasons be your inspiration: seasonal ingredients will be reasonably priced, widely available and at their flavorful best. This will also help you avoid a time-wasting search for one ingredient.

• Review the guest list for vegetarians and anyone with special dietary requirements, whether religious or medical.

• Provide something to please everybody. Be sure to consider both your more and your less adventurous guests. Include some old fashioned hors d'oeuvre classics as well as some creative new ones.

• Take into account how the ingredients are prepared, whether grilled, fried, baked, roasted, or raw, and try to achieve a good balance.

• Aim for a varied mix of ingredients and try not to repeat the same ingredient more than once in a menu.

• Include at least 2 hot hors d'oeuvres for parties during the colder months of the year.

THE QUANTITIES

A range of different factors play a part in how much your guests will eat. Hors d'oeuvre consumption goes up and down in direct relation to when, where, and who.

TIME OF YEAR: we are heartier eaters in the colder months.

TIME OF DAY: consider when your guests will have last eaten a full meal. Guests who have had to travel or have arrived straight from the office to a party will eat more.

LOCATION: a crowded space makes serving difficult and, as a result, reduces the quantities consumed.

GUESTS: friends and family will not be afraid to tuck in at a casual gathering, whereas a formal occasion makes everyone more reserved and, as a result, they tend to eat less. At charity events, where the guests have paid for their invitation, value for the money will be an issue and as a result people will expect there to be more food served.

The following quantities are only general guidelines, but can be a useful tool for menu planning.

Our basic rule is to allow 6 pieces per guest for the first hour and 4 pieces for each additional hour that the party continues.

For **pre-lunch or dinner drinks**, allow 3 pieces per guest and choose 3 different hors d'oeuvres.

For **hors d'oeuvres served instead of a first course before a lunch or dinner party**, allow 5 pieces per guest and choose 5 different hors d'oeuvres.

For a **2–3 hour cocktail party**, allow 10 pieces per guest and choose 5–10 different hors d'oeuvres.

For an hors d'oeuvres **only party served in place of a meal**, allow 14 pieces per guest and choose either 7 or 14 different hors d'oeuvres.

For a **stand-up wedding reception**, allow 12 pieces per guest and choose 8–10 different savory hors d'oeuvres and 2–4 different sweet hors d'oeuvres.

Focus on doing less better. We prefer to offer a smaller range of different kinds of hors d'oeuvres in a greater quantity. The finished product will be superior and you will save on time and cost. We recommend if you want to serve 10 hors d'oeuvres per guest to choose 5 different recipes and double the quantities.

THE STRATEGY

Parties are to enjoy—and that goes for you as well as your guests. A party at home is more relaxed when you are well organized. Planning is everything.

• Make two shopping lists, one for dry goods and nonperishable ingredients that can be purchased in advance, and another for foods that must be bought fresh the day before the party.

• Think through each recipe and make a cooking timetable. List all the stages of preparation, from complete recipes suitable for freezing to any last minute garnishing that needs to be done just before serving.

• Prepare ingredients and cook ahead as much as possible so you have plenty of time to complete the final preparations without suffering from party day panic. Use the THINK-AHEAD advice provided for each recipe in the book.

• Enlist family and friends, or hire professionals, to help you serve.

• Take stock of your serving dishes before the day of the party. Make sure you have enough and make arrangements to buy, borrow, or rent if necessary.

THE PRESENTATION

GENERAL RULES

Hors d'oeuvres must be tempting to the eye as well as pleasing to the palate. If food looks fabulous, people will feel confident that it tastes fabulous too. Follow these tips for beautiful, mouthwatering results.

• Arrange one, or at most two, kinds of hors d'oeuvres on a serving tray at a time. Too many kinds is not only visually confusing, but impractical, since guests have to break the flow of conversation to make their choice.

• Place hors d'oeuvres in neat, evenly spaced rows to maximize their aesthetic appeal.

• Odd numbers look better than even numbers, and diagonal lines are more pleasing to the eye than straight ones. Remember this golden rule of food presentation when arranging hors d'oeuvres on a serving tray.

• Don't crowd the serving trays. A densely packed arrangement can look cluttered and messy rather than generous.

• Keep garnishes simple. Over decorated food can look fussy and unappetizing.

• Make sure your guests have somewhere to put skewers or shells after they have finished eating an hors d'oeuvres.

• Avoid plates and platters that will be heavy or difficult to pass.

• Get help assembling hors d'oeuvres and arranging garnishes and trays. These final preparations are great fun when shared with family and friends.

• Have more napkins on hand than you think you'll need. When offering food, always have cocktail napkins handy for any guests who might need one.

NATURAL CONTAINERS AND GARNISHES

Fresh, edible garnishes are a simple, natural way to decorate (see pages 156–57).

Use brightly colored fruits and vegetables to garnish platters and trays. Hollow them out to make edible containers for nibbles, dippers, and dips. A serrated knife and a melon baller (see page 14) are essential tools for this. Prepare edible decorations up to 1 day in advance and store covered with damp paper towels in an airtight container in the refrigerator.

CREATIVE SERVING IDEAS

Innovative presentation doesn't have to be expensive and always makes food memorable and for some, even more delicious (see pages 158–159).

Fresh herbs make natural sticks for skewering (see page 148), fragrant bouquets for garnishing and an aromatic lining for a serving tray. Choose herbs unlikely to wilt, like rosemary, thyme, oregano, bay, lemon grass, and sage.

Use leaves to line trays or platters. Be sure to wipe fresh leaves clean with a damp cloth. Banana, fig, vine, palm, and cabbage leaves of all colors are ideal. Dried leaves, such as chestnut or lotus, should be brushed with sunflower oil before using.

Visit Asian and other ethnic stores for unusual but inexpensive serving ideas. A bamboo steamer used as a serving dish, chopsticks as skewers, sushi mats and noodles to line trays: these are all easy and inexpensive ways to add style to the presentation of an Asian-themed hors d'oeuvre menu. Use your imagination to come up with ideas of your own.

STATIONARY HORS D'OEUVRES

Hors d'oeuvre parties are an easy way to entertain a large number of people at home. Think, no chairs, no plates, no cutlery! If you are expecting more than 15 guests, you will need helping hands, be they hired professionals or recruits from family and friends. But not all the food has to be passed around on trays. A less formal approach is to arrange everything on stationary platters, trays, bowls and baskets. Place them on tables around the room and allow people to serve themselves.

NATURAL CONTAINERS AND GARNISHES

(1) MINIATURE PINEAPPLES: Use whole to decorate a stationary arrangement of hors d'oeuvres.

(2) NAVEL ORANGE: Julienne peel to garnish sweet or savory hors d'oeuvres.

(3) SWEET RED PEPPER: Hollow out to hold dips and sauces.

(4) SMALL EGGPLANT: Use whole to decorate a serving tray.

(5) BUTTERNUT SQUASH: Hollow out to hold vegetable dippers.

(6) ITALIAN PEPPER: Use whole to decorate a serving tray of spicy hors d'oeuvres.

(7) STAR FRUIT: Slice to garnish a serving tray of sweet hors d'oeuvres.

(8) FRESH MELON: Hollow out to hold fruit skewers and dipping sauces.

(9) PURPLE AND WHITE CABBAGE: Hollow out to use as a container for dips.

(10) LIMES AND LEMONS: Peel and segment to garnish individual hors d'oeuvres.

CREATIVE SERVING IDEAS

1. WICKER BASKET: To serve stacked hors d'oeuvres (see page 132).

2. SUSHI MAT: To line a serving tray (see page 90).

3. BANANA LEAVES: To line a serving tray (see page 73).

4. COARSE SEA SALT: To support shellfish hors d'oeuvres (see page 104).

5. BAMBOO STEAMER: To serve Asian-style hors d'oeuvres.

6. CHOP STICKS: As an alternative to wooden skewers (see page 71).

7. SOBA NOODLES: To line a serving tray (see page 94).

8. LEMON GRASS STALKS: To skewer grilled chicken (see page 74).

9. WOODEN TOOTHPICKS: To skewer bite-sized hors d'oeuvres (see page 68).

10. WOODEN SKEWERS

11. WOVEN TABLE MAT

12. SLATTED WOODEN TRAY

13. ROSEMARY SPRIG SKEWERS (see page 71).

MENU SUGGESTIONS

(see the index for page numbers)

DO NOTHING ON THE DAY

Consult this list for hors d'oeuvres that keep you out of the kitchen on the day of the party. All of them can be made at least 1 day ahead and transferred from storage container to serving tray with minimal effort.

Parmesan and Anchovy Palmiers
Cherry and Almond Frangipane Tartlets
Chorizo Puffs
Citrus Ginger Cream Tartlets
Creamy Blue Cheese and Scallion Dip
Crispy Potato Skins
Crunchy Sweet and Spicy Pecans
Curry Puffs
Curry Spiced Yogurt, Cilantro, and Mango Chutney Dip
Ham and Dijon Mini Croissants
Egg, Caper, and Cress Finger Sandwiches
Herbed Yogurt Dip
Herbed Pita Crisps
Honey Mustard and Prosciutto Palmiers
Mediterranean Marinated Olives
Mini Gougères
Queen Olive Cheese Balls
Oven-Dried Root and Fruit Chips
Rare Roast Beef and Horseradish Mayonnaise Finger Sandwiches
Roasted Red Pepper, Feta, and Mint Dip
Rolled Smoked Ham Crepes with Tarragon and Mustard Cream
Rolled Ricotta and Sage Crepes with Parmesan Shavings
Salsa Romesco Dip
Savory Sables
Smoked Salmon and Chive Cream Finger Sandwiches
Smoked Salmon Rugalach
Smoked Salmon Sushi Rice Balls
Spicy Peanut Dip
Spinach, Smoked Trout, and Herbed Cream Roulades
Spiced Party Nuts
Spiced Roasted Eggplant Dip
Sun-dried Tomato and Cannellini Bean Dip
Sun-dried Tomato Pesto Palmiers
Swiss Cheese Allumettes
Texas Red Bean Wraps with Cilantro Crema
Vegetable Dippers

HORS D'OEUVRES FROM THE GRILL

Let your guests mingle over some tasty nibbles while the barbecue heats up. Follow with food hot off the grill. Finish with a decadent dessert.

Crunchy Sweet and Spicy Pecans
Herbed Yogurt Dip with Crispy Potato Skins
Clams with Ginger and Lime Butter
Ginger Hoisin Chicken Drumsticks
Lemon Chili Shrimp Sticks
Curried Coconut Chicken Sticks
Quesadilla Triangles with Hot Pepper Relish
Strawberry and Pistachio Mini Meringues

LIGHT BITES FOR AL FRESCO ENTERTAINING

A midsummer menu for a lively party under the hot midday sun—serve in place of a first course, or double up the quantities and make it a meal.

Chilled Spiced Chickpea Soup with Avocado Salsa
Tomato and Basil Crostini
Basil Marinated Mozzarella and Cherry Tomato Skewers
Radish Cups with Black Olive Tapenade
Mini Peking Duck Pancakes with Plum Sauce

CELEBRATION BRUNCH FOR THE FAMILY

Classic hors d'oeuvres for a brunch party appeal to young and old alike. Perfect with your favorite fruit juice, everything but the croque monsieur can be prepared a day ahead and assembled well in advance.

Ham and Dijon Mini Croissants
Egg and Bacon Puffs
Mini Croque Monsieur
Baby Bagels with Cream Cheese, Lox, and Dill
Rosemary Mini Muffins with Smoked Ham and Peach Relish
Tiny Dill Scones with Smoked Trout and Horseradish Cream
Tropical Fruit Brochettes with Passion Fruit and Mascarpone Dip

ELEGANT APPETIZERS FOR A SHORT FORMAL RECEPTION

Prelude to an elegant evening of entertaining—many of these can be started ahead, but you will need an extra pair of hands just before serving to help with the final touches.

Chive-Tied Crepe Bundles with Smoked Salmon and Lemon Crème Fraîche
Tarragon and Mustard Lobster Bouchées
Baby Baked Potatoes with Sour Cream and Caviar
Asparagus Croutes with Lemon Hollandaise
Carpaccio Canapés

FAST AND FABULOUS MENU

Good food in a hurry—use the THINK AHEAD notes to get the dip and crostini finished before guests arrive. Grill the chicken and shrimp sticks to order. You've done it!

Creamy Blue Cheese and Scallion Dip with Herbed Pita Crisps
Avocado and Goat Cheese Crostini
Curried Coconut Chicken Sticks
Tangy Thai Shrimp Skewers

PORTABLE HORS D'OEUVRES FOR AN EVENING IN THE PARK

A varied menu that can be completely prepared in advance and transported easily—bring along wicker baskets, wooden bowls, and large napkins and arrange the food when you arrive at the perfect spot.

Swiss Cheese Allumettes
Salsa Romesco Dip with
    Vegetable Dippers
Mini Pissaladiere
Spicy Pork Empanaditas with Chunky
    Avocado Relish
Roasted Red Onion and Thyme
    Foccacine
Minted Feta and Pine Nut Filo Rolls
    with Lemon Aioli
Triple Chocolate Biscottini with
    Hazelnuts

CANDELIGHT WINTER WEDDING AT HOME

A welcoming, warming menu of traditional hors d'oeuvres with a twist—we recommend starting the preparation two days in advance; refer to the THINK AHEAD notes.

Carrot, Honey, and Ginger Soup Cups
Cocktail Salmon and Dill Cakes with
    Crème Fraîche Tartare
Portobello Mushroom and
    Hollandaise Tartlets
Orange Muffins with Smoked Turkey
    and Cranberry Sauce
Filo Tartlets with Smoked Salmon,
    Cracked Pepper, and Lime
Quail Egg, Caviar, and Chervil
    Croustades
Grilled Beef Fillet with Salsa
    Verde Croutes
Chive Pancakes with Crème Fraîche
    and Red Onion Confit
Cherubs on Horseback
Mini Mango Galettes
Bittersweet Chocolate Tartlets
Mini Sticky Orange and
    Almond Cakes

MEDITERRANEAN FEAST

A big on flavor, make ahead menu for a special occasion.

Parmesan and Pine Nut Biscottini
    with Green Olives
Sundried Tomato and Cannellini Bean
    Dip with Herbed Pita Crisps
Spicy Shrimp Crostini
Artichoke and Gorgonzola Focaccine
Feta, Olive, and Rosemary Quichettes
Polenta Crostini with Tomato and
    Black Olive Salsa
Chicken, Prosciutto, and Sage
Spiedini with Roasted Pepper Aioli

TEMPTING TREATS FOR AN INFORMAL EVENING WITH FRIENDS

Simple and delicious food for a relaxing and enjoyable evening—everything can be made before your guests arrive. The skewers are the only last-minute item needing attention

Mediterranean Marinated Olives
Savory Sables
Roasted Red Pepper, Feta, and Mint
    Dip with Vegetable Dippers
Filo Tartlets with Spicy
    Cilantro Shrimp
Wild Rice and Scallion Pancakes
    with Avocado Lime Salsa
Sesame Soy Glazed Beef Skewers
Mini Chocolate Truffle Cake

VEGETARIAN HORS D'OEUVRES FOR A CROWD

Fabulous finger food without meat or fish—combine a range of vegetables with fragrant herbs, pungent cheeses, and crisp pastries to tempt even the most hardened of carnivores.

Olive Cheese Balls
Twisted Parsley Breadsticks
Lemon Marinated Tortellini and
    Sun-dried Tomato Skewers
Mini Cherry Tomato and Basil
    Pesto Galettes
Roasted Pepper, Goat Cheese, and
    Mint Wraps

Crispy Carrot and Scallion
    Cakes with Feta and Black Olive
Herbed Artichoke and Parmesan
    Filo Rolls with Light Lemon
    Mayonnaise Dip
Focaccine Pockets with Wild
    Mushrooms and Thyme
Eggplant and Pine Nut Fritters with
    Roasted Tomato Sauce
Polenta Crostini with Blue Cheese and
    Balsamic Red Onions

AFTERNOON TEA MENU FOR A SUMMER WEDDING

A mix of teatime classics and contemporary inspirations—this menu sets the scene for a truly memorable occasion. Read through the THINK AHEAD notes and begin preparation two days in advance.

Smoked Salmon and Chive Cream
    Finger Sandwiches
Egg, Caper, and Cress Finger
    Sandwiches
Gingered Chicken Cakes with
    Cilantro Lime Mayonnaise
Tiny Parmesan and Rosemary
    Shortbreads with Roasted Cherry
    Tomatoes and Feta
Valentine Cucumber Cream Canapés
Dill Pancakes with Salmon Caviar and
    Lemon Creme Fraiche
Rare Roast Beef with Wholegrain
    Mustard in Poppy Seed Tartlets
Snowpea Wrapped Shrimp Skewers
    with Lemon Mayonnaise
Filo Tartlets with Bang Bang Chicken
Cucumber Cups with Smoked Trout
    Mousse, Lemon, and Dill
Tiny Shortcakes with
    Strawberries and Cream
Mini Raspberry Ripple
Meringue Kisses

NOTES FROM THE COOKS ON THE INGREDIENTS

ANCHOVY FILLETS If you find the flavor of anchovies too pungent, you can soak them in milk for 10 minutes before using.

ARTICHOKE We use jars of baby globe artichoke hearts marinated in oil.

ARUGULA Long leaves and a peppery flavor. It is very perishable. Store tightly wrapped in a plastic bag in the refrigerator for up to 2 days.

AVOCADO A **small avocado** weighs about ⅛lb; a **medium avocado** weighs about ½lb; a **large avocado** weighs about ¾lb. Oxygen in the air turns avocado brown; pressing plastic wrap directly on the surface of an avocado dip will prevent it from turning.

BEETS A small beet weighs about ¼lb. To cook raw beets, bake unpeeled in a preheated 300°F oven until tender, 1 hour.

BREADCRUMBS To make **fresh breadcrumbs**, cut bread into slices, cut off crusts and cut into pieces. Place in a blender or food processor; pulse until finely ground. Store in an airtight container for up to 2 days.
To make **dried breadcrumbs**, cut day-old bread into slices, cut off the crusts. Bake in a preheated 300°F oven until dry and crisp, 10 minutes. Place in a blender or food processor; pulse until finely ground. Store in an airtight container for up to 1 month.

BUCKWHEAT FLOUR Gray-brown in color with a distinct bitter flavor; available at healthfood stores and in large supermarkets.

BUTTER For this book, butter means unsalted or lightly salted butter.

CAPERS The pickled bud of the caper plant. We use regular and baby ones (see page 13); always drain well before using.

CARDAMOM Best used freshly ground as its fragrance diminishes with time. Open, discard the seed pods and crush the black or brown seeds.

CAVIAR (see page 10). Salted fish roe (eggs) available in various qualities and at hugely varying prices. A little goes a long way.

CHEESE Fresh **creamy goat cheese** is a fresh, white, rindless, lightly sour cheese, available in rolls, rounds, or pyramids. As an alternative, combine 3 parts cream cheese with 1 part whole milk yogurt until smooth.
Danish Blue is a creamy, blue veined Danish blue cheese with a mild flavor. Use a mild blue cheese as an alternative.
Gorgonzola cheese is a rich, bluish green veined Italian cheese with a piquant flavor. Use a strong blue cheese as an alternative.
Gruyère cheese is a hard Swiss cheese with a sweet, nutty flavor. Unlike so many hard cheeses, it melts without becoming oily or rubbery. Use Emmenthal or a hard yellow cheese as an alternative.
Mascarpone cheese is a rich, velvety Italian cream cheese. As an alternative, mix 3 parts cream cheese with 1 part heavy cream and a pinch of sugar until smooth.
Parmesan cheese (see page 10) is an Italian hard cheese with a rich, sharp flavor that is nothing like the smelly, cheesy taste of grated Parmesan that is sold in a can. Always buy Parmesan by the piece and grate as required.
Roquefort cheese (see page 10) is a rich, creamy, green-veined French cheese made from sheep's milk with a piquant flavor. Use a strong blue cheese as an alternative.
Stilton cheese (see page 10) is a rich, crumbly bluish green veined British cheese with a pungent flavor. Use a strong blue cheese as an alternative.

CHERVIL A very delicately flavored herb; use flat-leaf (Italian) parsley as an alternative.

CHILI There are over 200 different varieties of fresh chilies, varying in color, size, shape, and heat. As a general rule, the smaller the chili the hotter it is. Capsaicin, the substance in chilies responsible for their heat, can cause a very painful burning sensation if it comes into contact with the eyes, mouth, or other sensitive skin. Make sure you wash your hands thoroughly after handling chilies, or wear rubber gloves. To reduce the level of heat, remove the seeds before using.
Crushed chilies (see page 12) are a widely available hot seasoning or can be made at home by crushing dried chilies in a mortar and pestle or an electric coffee grinder.
Chipotles in Adobo (see page 13) are dried smoked jalapeño chilies pickled and canned in a piquant sauce made from chilies, herbs, and vinegar. Available in some supermarkets, mail order, or from speciality stores.

CHILI SAUCE We use two different types: **Chinese hot chili sauce** (see page 12), made from chilies, salt, and vinegar; and **Thai sweet chili sauce** (see page 12), flavored with ginger and garlic as well as sugar, salt, vinegar, and chilies. Both available in large supermarkets or in Asian stores.

CHINESE PANCAKES Available chilled and frozen in Asian stores and large supermarkets.

CHIPOTLES IN ADOBO (see chilies).

CHORIZO Pork sausage flavored and colored with paprika, frequently used in Spanish and Mexican cooking. It can be mild or highly spiced. It is mostly available cured and can be eaten without cooking.

CREME FRAICHE Thick cream with a slightly sour flavor and a velvety texture. It keeps longer than ordinary cream and can be boiled without curdling. For cooking, substitute heavy cream. For garnishing, substitute equal parts of whipped heavy cream (see page 144) combined with whole milk yogurt or use sour cream.

COCONUT MILK We used canned cocunut milk, available at Asian stores and large supermarkets. Shake well before opening.

CORN Available fresh on the cob or as frozen or canned kernels. To cut kernels from the cob, stand the corn upright and carefully cut downward with a sharp knife.

CORN MEAL We use yellow, medium-ground cornmeal; use Italian polenta as an alternative.

CORNICHONS Crisp pickles made from tiny gherkin cucumbers; also called cocktail gherkins.

CRAB When buying cooked crab in the shell, choose one that feels heavy for its size. Whether bought fresh, canned, or frozen, cooked crabmeat should be picked over with your fingers to remove any membrane or pieces of shell.

DUMPLING WRAPPERS Small rounds of fresh noodle dough available fresh and frozen in Chinese stores or gourmet supermarkets. They can be stored in the refrigerator for up to 1 week if well wrapped.

EGGPLANT A medium eggplant weighs about ⅔ lb.

EGGS We use large in our recipes; 1 beaten egg is 3 tbsp beaten egg, 1 egg yolk is 1 tbsp egg yolk, and 1 egg white is 2 tbsp egg white. **Quail eggs** (see page 11) are available at Asian markets and in the gourmet section of large supermarkets. They are difficult to peel, so plunge them into cold water as soon as they are cooked and peel them at once under cold running water. Refrigerate them in water.

FIGS Best in season, in the late summer and early autumn months.

FISH SAUCE Thin, salty brown sauce made from fermented fish used extensively in Southeast Asian cooking. Available in large supermarkets and Asian stores. We use **Thai fish sauce** called *nam pla;* use light soy sauce as an alternative.

FIVE-SPICE POWDER A Chinese blend of ground cloves, cinnamon, fennel, star anise, and Szechuan peppercorns, available prepackaged in Asian markets and many supermarkets.

FRUIT in all of the recipes should be washed and, unless otherwise stated, also peeled.

GARLIC Unless we indicate otherwise, all garlic cloves are medium-sized.

GINGER Do not substitute ground ginger for **fresh ginger**; the flavors are quite different. Store fresh ginger wrapped in the refrigerator for up to 3 weeks. Cut off the skin with a sharp knife before measuring. **Preserved stem ginger** is fresh ginger preserved in jars in a thick syrup. **Candied Ginger** can be substituted. **Pickled ginger** (see page 12) is the Japanese condiment for sushi. It is easily recognized by its pink color; it is available in jars.

HAZELNUTS To skin hazelnuts, spread in a single layer in a large baking pan and bake in a preheated 350°F oven for about 10 minutes. Wrap the warm nuts in a coarse-textured dish towel and rub briskly to loosen the skin as much as possible.

HERBS in all of the recipes are always fresh, unless otherwise specified.

HOISIN SAUCE Slightly sweet, thick, dark brown sauce made from soy beans, garlic, and spices. Keeps indefinitely in a covered jar.

LEMON CURD Best homemade. Follow the method for making passion curd (see page 127), but use ⅔ cup lemon juice and 1 tsp grated lemon zest instead of the passion fruit and lemon-juice mixture.

LEMON GRASS Long, grasslike herb with a strong citrus flavor and aroma. Use only the tender inner stalk since the outer leaves are tough. Use a mixture of grated lime and lemon peel as an alternative.

MANGO To slice or dice a fresh mango, find where the flat side of the large seed is by rolling the mango on a work surface; it will settle on a flat side. Cut the peeled mango lengthwise on both sides of the seed so the knife just misses it. Put each mango piece cut side down and cut it lengthwise into slices, dice if required.

MASA HARINA Finely ground cornmeal treated with lime used to make corn tortillas; available mail order and in speciality stores.

MIRIN Japanese rice wine, sweeter than sake and used only for cooking. Use medium dry sherry as an alternative.

MUSHROOMS To clean mushrooms, be sure never to wash directly in water but, instead, wipe them with damp paper towels. **Portobello mushrooms** have an open, flat cap with exposed brown gills and a strong, savory flavor. **Shiitake mushrooms** are an Asian variety with a powerful meaty flavor. There are many varieties of **wild mushrooms**; our favorites are chanterelles, porcini (also called cepes), and morels. Field or shiitake mushrooms can be used as an alternative.

MUSTARD (see page 13). We prefer French Dijon mustard; It is available ground completely smooth or as **grainy mustard which** is made from crushed mustard seeds. **Dried mustard** is one of the strongest and hottest of mustards.

NORI Sold in paper thin sheets. It is an edible seaweed that is a popular flavoring and garnish in Japanese cooking.

ONIONS When called for in the book, an onion is a yellow onion. A **medium red onion** weighs about ¼ lb. A **Spanish onion** is a large, mild yellow onion. When we ask for a **scallion**, we mean both the green and white parts, unless otherwise specified. A **shallot** has a more subtle flavor than a yellow onion.

OYSTERS Ask your fish dealer to shuck the oysters for you; cover and refrigerate for up to 2 days. Smoked oysters are available in cans.

PANCETTA Flavorful Italian streaky bacon. Store wrapped in the refrigerator for up to 3 weeks. Use regular bacon as an alternative.

PARSLEY We use flat-leaf (also called Italian) parsley in all recipes.

PASSION FRUIT Choose wrinkled passion fruit as they are riper and therefore more sweet and juicy.

POLENTA Made from ground corn, but is slightly courser in texture and more golden in color than medium cornmeal. Use course cornmeal as an alternative.

POMEGRANATE Only in season during the winter months. Choose fruits with a bright yellow skin streaked with bright pink. Store in the refrigerator for up to 3 weeks.

PROSCIUTTO (see page 10) Italian raw ham that has been seasoned, salt-cured, and air-dried.

RICE PAPERS Dried brittle translucent sheets made from rice flour. Available in Asian markets, they keep indefinitely.

SAFFRON The world's most expensive spice. Choose saffron threads rather than saffron powder.

SALT Always use sea salt, whether coarse or fine.

SAKE Japan's famous rice wine is widely used as a flavoring in Japanese sauces and marinades. Use dry sherry as an alternative.

SCALLOPS Bay scallops (see page 11) are about ¼-inch across. Sea scallops (see page 11) are larger but vary in size. For hors d'oeuvres, choose sea scallops about 2 inches across.

SESAME We use Asian brands of sesame oil that are extracted from toasted sesame seeds. A lighter oil with a less intense flavor is also available in healthfood stores. Sesame seeds are widely used as flavoring in Chinese and Japanese cooking.

SHALLOT (see onion).

SHRIMP (see page 11). To devein shrimp, cut off the heads and peel away the shells and legs. With a sharp knife, cut along the top of each shrimp and pull out the black vein. Wash and dry well.

SOBA NOODLES Very fine Japanese buckwheat noodles (see page 156).

SOY SAUCE Major seasoning in Asian cooking, available in a number of varieties ranging in color and flavor. We use light soy sauce when we want to preserve the color of the food but dark soy sauce imparts a richer flavor. Japanese soy sauce called *shoyu* is sweeter, lighter, and less salty; use light soy sauce as an alternative.

SUGAR Any white sugar (whether superfine or granulated) that you have on hand.

SUGAR CANE Available fresh, frozen, and canned, at Asian and Caribbean markets. When buying canned, read the label to be sure the can contains sugarcane sticks and not chopped sugarcane

TAHINI Paste made from grinding roasted sesame seeds and sold in jars in large supermarkets and Middle Eastern markets. Shake well before using.

TOMATO For fresh tomatoes we mean either round or plum and always red and ripe. Let unripe tomatoes ripen on a window sill for a few days. Canned tomatoes are peeled, chopped plum tomatoes. Tomato sauce is tomatoes that are strained completely smooth. Tomato paste refers to concentrated, cooked tomatoes, available in cans or tubes. Sundried tomatoes are marinated in jars in oil; drain before using.

VEGETABLES Washed and, unless otherwise stated, peeled in all recipes.

VINEGAR Red-wine vinegar and white-wine vinegar have different flavors and levels of acidity and should not be used interchangeably. Balsamic vinegar (see page 12) is dark in color with a sweet, pungent flavor. Use red-wine vinegar sweetened with a pinch of sugar as an alternative. Rice vinegar with its subtly sweet, mellow flavor is used extensively in Japanese cooking. White-wine vinegar sweetened with a pinch of sugar can be used as an alternative but not for flavoring sushi rice. In this case no substitution can be made.

WASABI Pungent green horseradish used in Japanese cuisine. It is available in a dried powder form in cans and as a paste in tubes.

WHOLE MILK YOGURT Made from cow's or sheep's milk and is especially rich, creamy, and flavorful. Use a mixture of 1 part plain nonfat yogurt and 1 part sour cream as an alternative.

AUTHORS' ACKNOWLEDGMENTS

We would like to thank:
Three very special **Books for Cooks** cooks for their generosity and expertise. Kim Barber for her indispensible sushi masterclass and for letting us include her fabulous Sushi Rice Balls in the book. Jennifer Joyce for lending us her Southwestern and Pacific hors d'oeuvres recipes. Ursula Ferrigno for allowing us to miniaturize her Red Onion Schiacatta and Eggplant Polpette. Heidi Lascelles, founder and proprietor of Books for Cooks, for supporting us in all our ventures, whether writing books, teaching classes, moving house, or having a baby.

Juliet Kindersley, for a mother's love, care and understanding. And for the loan of her kitchen, in which many of the recipes were tried and tested. James Middlehurst, for giving us the green light. Baby Frances, for letting us borrow her mummy. Her mummy Julia Pemberton Hellums for being just great, again.

And most of all, Stuart Jackman. For giving us a chance. For making it happen.

MAIL-ORDER SOURCES

US

ADRIANA'S CARAVAN
409 Vanderbilt Street
Brooklyn, NY 11218
800-316-0820
www.adrianascaravan.com
Catalog available. Herbs, spices, condiments, and ethnic ingredients from around the world.

CHEF'S
PO Box 620048
Dallas, TX 75262
800-338-3232
www.chefscatalog.com
Catalog available. Professional restaurant equipment for the home chef.

DEAN & DELUCA
560 Broadway
New York, NY 10012
800-221-7714
www.dean-deluca.com
Catalog available. Luxury ingredients and specialty foods from around the world.

GOURMETSLEUTH
Gourmetsleuth
PO Box 508
Los Gatos, CA 95031
408-354-8281
www.gourmetsleuth.com
Online provider of tools for the cook, ethnic spices and more.

KATAGIRI
224 East 59th Street
New York, NY 10016
212-683-4419
www.katagiri.com
Japanese specialty ingredients.

MING'S PANTRY
www.mingspantry.com
Online provider of Chinese and Asian food products, including hot chile sauces and rice vinegar.

PENDERY'S
www.penderys.com
Online provider of chiles and spices and other Latin American food products.

PENZEYS SPICES
PO Box 933
Muskego, WI 53150
414-679-7207
www.penzeys.com
Catalog available. Herbs, spices, and seasonings.

SUR LA TABLE
Catalog Division
1765 Sixth Avenue South
Seattle, Washington 98134
800-243-0852
www.surlatable.com
Catalog available. Tools for the cook.

CANADA

EPICUREAN FOODS
www.epicureanfoods.com/ca
1-800-267-0805
Online provider of gourmet foods.

PASHA-GOURMET
9 Nelson Ave.
Outremont QC H2V3Z5
Canada
(514) 948-5442
www.pasha-gourmet.com
Gourmet foods and spices.

A Cook's Tools and Techniques
#250 - 16th Street
West Vancouver, BC V7V 3R5
Canada
604.925.1835
www.thestoreforcooks.com
Cooking accessories.